Almost a Statistic: The R
Drs. Vickie and Ma

As told to
Jessica Wallace McBride, Ph.D.

M Millennium International
Publishing Group

ISBN 978-0-578-15674-3

Events, locales, and conversations have been recreated from the memories of the subjects. In order to maintain their anonymity, in some instances the names of individuals and places have been changed along with some identifying characteristics and details such as physical properties, occupations and places of residence.

Cover photograph © 2014 Maurice McBride
Cover design by Maurice McBride and Jessica Wallace McBride
Interior photographs provided by Vickie McBride and Maurice McBride
Editing support provided by Alfreda W. Lewis and Barbara Joe Williams
Book design and production by Millennium International Publishing Group
Author photograph provided by Jessica Wallace McBride

Dedication

To Alfreda W. Lewis
God couldn't have given me a better mother.
I appreciate you and love you forever.
-JWM

Table of Contents

Preface

On August 10, 2013, Vickie and Maurice McBride became the first parent and child in history to earn their doctorates from the same school on the same day. Maurice crossed the stage at Capella University's commencement first, earning a Ph.D. in Organization and Management. Vickie crossed the same stage minutes later, earning a Ph.D. in K-12 Studies in Education. The following month, Vickie and Maurice's story went global. First, their amazing journey was detailed in *The True Citizen*, local newspaper of their hometown, Waynesboro, Georgia. A few weeks later, this mother and son were featured on WRDW News 12, the local CBS station in neighboring Augusta, Georgia. Within a few days, their story had gone viral, appearing on· websites including huffingtonpost.com, msnNOW.com, blackamericaweb.com, and newsone.com. At the end of 2013, theirs was recognized as one of the "Most Inspirational Stories of 2013" by Black Entertainment Television (www.bet.com).

This book is the result of the many inquiries from people who were inspired by Vickie and Maurice's story, and wanted to know more about how they avoided limiting themselves to others' low expectations and becoming statistics. Dr. Vickie McBride continues to be an inspiration for all mothers who are determined to persevere, despite the daunting challenges and discouraging attitudes they face. Dr. Maurice McBride will always represent for the people who make bad decisions and errors in judgment, and have to fight for years to escape from the shadows of their mistakes. This "Dynamic Duo," as they were dubbed in the February 2014 edition of *Ebony* magazine, is living proof that, with love, support, and patience, anyone who is willing to put forth the effort can succeed.

The content of this work of creative nonfiction was collected during a year-long period. It is the telling of events from the perspectives of the subjects, and the events, dialogue, and places are portrayed to the best of their memories. While all the content in this book is true according to the subjects' recollection, some names and identifying details have been changed to protect the privacy of the people involved. I encourage everyone to read this book without rendering judgment or placing blame.

Drs. Vickie and Maurice McBride are available for speaking engagements. If interested, they may be contacted via email at dr.mcbrideexperience@gmail.com.

It is my honor to have been chosen to tell this powerful story.

Jessica Wallace McBride, Ph.D.
Savannah, Georgia
December 2014

Chapter 1
Thank God the Couch Is Green

Vickie

"Dr. Maurice McBride."

I applaud as my first born son crosses the stage. Unlike most parents who are seated in the audience far away from their children during this proud moment, I am seated just a few rows behind Maurice as he is hooded and shakes hands with Scott Kinney, the president of Capella University; the commencement speaker; and others. Since Mr. Kinney had shared our story at the beginning of the commencement exercises, everyone clapped when they heard Maurice's name, but I could still hear his fiancé's excited cheer above the applause. A short while before, I had sent her a text message thanking her for helping and supporting both of us through this process. If there was anyone whose pride came close to matching mine at this moment, it was hers. As I watch Maurice duck to allow the hood to be placed over his head, the broad grin on his face brings a smile to mine, and I can feel the tears of joy threatening to spill as fellow graduates seated near me offered their congratulations. The tears are quickly replaced by a laugh when Maurice, true to form, dances his way across the stage after being hooded. *That's my child,* I think. *Always the performer.* Put him in front of an audience and you are guaranteed a show.

As Maurice takes his seat and I wait on my turn to cross the same stage and shake the same hands, my mind is inundated with memories of his life and my struggle as a child raising a child. Just a few years before, if anyone had told me that I would see Maurice graduate with the highest degree attainable, I honestly would not have believed it. The smiling faces around us have only a general idea about my son's personal battles, and my struggle to raise him. He was my trouble child. My *troubled* child. The one I worried about the most and prayed for the hardest. The one who I fought to keep when my mother wanted me to put him up for adoption,

1

fought with when he defied me, and fought for when others mistreated him.

When Maurice was a toddler, I started to see behavior problems. Since I was such a young mother, my mother, Mattie Lee McBride, was raising both of us and didn't really take my input too seriously. We often battled over parenting Maurice because, young or not, I was his mother, not his sister, and I wanted my voice in his upbringing to be respected. Even when it became clear that there were going to be challenges, I wasn't allowed to teach him any responsibilities. Mama would not require him to do the simplest things, like pick up after himself; would not hold him accountable at all, no matter what he did; and gave him anything and everything he wanted. He became increasingly defiant and his sense of entitlement grew. Neither Mama nor I could predict the ways in which this unchecked attitude would cost him (and us) later in life. I saw it sooner than she did, and by the time she was aware of the severity of the problem, it was too late.

Maurice and I began our lives together in February of 1975. I was 13 years old - a typical junior high school student who liked spending time with my friends and playing the trumpet in the marching band. Like most other girls whose families could afford it, I had taken piano lessons from the local piano teacher, Mrs. Jones, for several years, but stopped as I got older and my interests changed. My only sibling was a much older brother named Don who also played the trumpet, so I was raised like an only child for much of my childhood. In fact, I had just recently started sleeping in my own bed by this age, often preferring to sleep with my mother.

One day, my junior high school band went to the senior high school to practice in their band room. While we were over there, I saw one of my best friends, Bonita, talking to an older boy. I thought he was cute, and I asked Bonita who he was.

"That's my brother, Phillip," she told me.

"Well, I like your brother," I said.

"He has a girlfriend," she informed me.

I didn't pursue it any further. I knew I wasn't allowed to have a boyfriend and rarely even talked to boys, so this was nothing more than a school girl crush. The high schooler with a girlfriend would just remain my friend's cute older brother.

During those days, parents didn't talk to their children the way they do now. I literally knew nothing about boys. In fact, I didn't know anything about anything. Children simply were not raised in the highly sexualized environment that is common today. Not only was this the 1970s, but it was small town Georgia and I was being raised by a woman who, after having three miscarriages, had adopted me as an infant when she was in her mid-50s. When I started my period at age ten, I had no idea what was happening. I didn't tell my mama because I didn't know there was anything to tell. She discovered it by keeping a close eye on the laundry, and then sat me down to talk. After a few questions, she determined that I had started my period. The rest of the conversation went something like this:

Mama: "Baby, don't mess with boys."

Me: "Okay."

By age 13, I had reached my full adult height of five feet two inches and was fully developed. I was completely unaware of my physicality, however. My development wasn't a positive or negative thing, and I don't remember anyone, male or female, really making it an issue. My mother kept me dressed in conservative, age appropriate clothes, and my hair was usually in an afro. I had no thought of going against her instructions to not "mess with boys." If boys were attracted to me, I was unaware of it.

A few days or weeks after seeing Bonita's brother Phillip at the high school, I walked to my cousin Charles' house to hang out. His mother, Sammie Joe, and my mother were sisters who talked daily and often shopped together, usually with me in tow. In the days before malls, Aunt Sammie Joe, Mama, and I would go to downtown Augusta, Georgia, about 30 miles away and walk up one side of Broad Street and down the other, going into every single store along the way. Inevitably, we ended up back in the very first store we visited for Aunt Sammie Joe to purchase the first item she had looked at hours before. Spending my Saturdays like this is probably why I've always hated shopping.

Even though my cousin Charles was older than me, he and I got along well and it wasn't unusual for us to spend time together. When I visited that day, Phillip was there. I didn't know they were friends. He introduced himself and the three of us talked for a few minutes before Charles left to go to another friend's house, leaving me alone with Phillip since my aunt wasn't at home.

"Come talk to me," Phillip said. We were both in the den, so I sat down on the other end of the couch in response to his request. "Do you have a boyfriend?" he asked.

"No, I'm too young to have a boyfriend," I told him. I had no desire to go against my mother's rules. "Besides, Bonita said that you have a girlfriend."

"I'll leave her alone if you'll be my girlfriend," he said as he placed his hand on my thigh. I was wearing shorts and a shirt - nondescript play clothes - so his hand was on my skin. *Uh oh.* I didn't know that he was running game on a thirteen-year-old girl, but his hand on my thigh was a red flag. I knew something wasn't right by the way he looked at me, and I realized I had to get out of there.

I moved away, but he didn't remove his hand. "I have to go," I said, and stood up. I couldn't really explain it, and I didn't know what his intentions were, but I could feel that something was wrong and that I needed to leave.

"Have you kissed a boy?" he asked, ignoring my statement.

"No," I told him truthfully. I headed to the living room so I could leave through the front door. Aunt Sammie Joe's living room was decorated with Victorian furniture similar to what we had in our living room at home.

"Where are you going? Sit back down," Phillip told me. I kept walking. By this point, I was starting to get scared and my mind was racing to find a way out of this situation. Phillip followed me to the front room and when I turned to face him, he grabbed me by both wrists. "I'm going to teach you how to kiss a boy."

He sat me down next to him on my aunt's green Victorian sofa, leaned in, and kissed me. I didn't like it and leaned back to get away from him. When I did that, he positioned himself on top of me. By now, I knew something was *very* wrong. The look in his eyes was one I had never seen before, and his grip on my arms, though not painful, was firm enough to let me know I wasn't going to be able to fight my way out of this.

"I need to go home," I told him. "Get off of me!" He didn't respond. Still, I tried to leave, but I was no physical match for him. I was struck by fear and overwhelmed by the powerlessness that I felt. "Get up! Get off me! You're hurting me! Let me go!" I said over and over again. He ignored my pleas.

"This won't take long," he said as he kept me pinned to the sofa. Still, I struggled to get free and begged to be let go as he pulled down my shorts and underwear. My heart was racing, and I was filled with fright. I was helpless against this bigger, stronger, older boy. As I struggled to stop him from doing whatever he was trying to do, I felt him push into me.

"Stop! Don't do that! No! Let me go!" I cried, but it was useless. The people who would help me couldn't hear me, and the person who could hear me didn't care. I cannot describe the pain I felt pinned to that green Victorian sofa being violated by Bonita's older brother and my cousin's friend. I knew he was having sex with me, and I knew it was wrong. I fought as hard as I could, but I lost.

When Phillip was done, he said, "I'm sorry. I didn't mean to hurt you." He got off of me and dressed himself. "We have to clean up. Where are the towels?" he asked. I couldn't move. I couldn't speak. I couldn't cry. Something bad had happened, and I just didn't know what to do, so I lay there, stiff and mute as he rummaged around the house for towels.

After a few moments, I was able to get up and get dressed. The blood and bodily fluid that soiled the green sofa also stained my clothes. Phillip tried to wipe off the couch with the towels he found, but he could not remove the dark stain. He continued to apologize to me as he tried to remove all evidence of what he had done, but he got no response. Eventually, he walked out of the house, leaving me hurt and alone.

How am I going to get home? I thought as I stood by myself in the living room. After a few seconds, I decided to walk home and hoped that no one would see me or talk to me. On the way, I ignored the pain between my legs and replayed the day's events in my head. *Thank God the couch is green*, I thought. At least no one would see my blood and I wouldn't get in trouble for messing up my aunt's Victorian sofa. I didn't know what I was going to tell my mama because I didn't have the words to describe what had happened. I didn't know much, but I knew Phillip had sex with me, and I had no idea how to tell her this without getting in trouble. On that solitary walk home, I decided to hide what had happened to me; I really didn't see another option. When I got there, I bathed immediately and put a maxi pad in my clean pair of panties. I threw my shorts and underwear away and went about my regular routine until it was time for bed. I just wanted everything to be normal.

In school the next day, I decided to tell Bonita what happened. "Guess what," I said when I saw her.

"What?" she asked.

"I had sex with your brother." I don't know why I told her; I suppose I just needed for someone else to know what happened, or at least know a part of what happened. I couldn't call it rape; that word wasn't even known to me.

"For real?" she asked in shock. I nodded my confirmation, and she shook her head. "That's just the way he is," she told me. We left it at that.

Eventually, my mother noticed that I hadn't had a period in two months. She asked me about it, but I didn't have any answers. I didn't know why I had missed two periods but still had the symptoms I usually had, like sore breasts. When I told her as much, she made an appointment for me to see our family physician, Dr. Bynes.

"Why are we here?" I asked when we arrived at his office. I didn't get much of a response. As I said, being raised in the 1970s by a woman in her late 60s in small town Georgia meant that children didn't always get answers. Still, I inquired. After Dr. Bynes examined me and left the room, I asked Mama, "Why did he look down there?" I had been on an examination table with my feet in stirrups for the first time, and wanted answers. Still, I got nothing. I was only told to get dressed. Afterwards, I sat down with Mama and the doctor.

Even though I was the one who had been examined, Dr. Bynes spoke to my mother, addressing her by a shortened version of her first name. "Matt Lee, her cervix is soft. Go on home and I'll call you when I know more." I didn't know what a cervix was, so I didn't know how to feel about mine being soft, or if I should feel any way at all. On the ride home, Mama and I were quiet. I knew it wouldn't help to ask questions, and I can only imagine what was going through her mind.

Later that afternoon, the phone rang. I answered it in the kitchen and told Mama that Dr. Bynes wanted to speak to her. She picked up the receiver in her room, and I stayed on the line in the kitchen. After cordial greetings, Dr. Bynes got right to business. "Matt Lee, she's pregnant."

The next thing I remember is being helped up off of the floor. When I regained consciousness, Mama told me I had fainted. Amazingly, she was calm. She sat me next to her on her bed and asked, "Vickie, have you been messing with any boys?"

"No," I answered her honestly. I had never done any such thing. What Phillip had done to me had been tucked neatly away in my mind, and I had tried so hard to forget it that I almost had. Burying painful things would become a habit.

"You had to, Vickie."

"Why?" I asked.

"Because you're pregnant," she answered.

What does one have to do with the other? I wondered.

"You don't have to tell me now," Mama continued, "but you will need to tell me eventually. Go in your room and think about it."

I did as I was told. *Pregnant.* I was numb. How in the world could I be pregnant? I never messed with boys. I didn't even know that boys had anything to do with babies! I sat on my bed

7

wondering how in the world this could have happened. And then I remembered. *Phillip*. He was a boy, and I figured he had "messed with" me by having sex with me, and that's what did it. I went back to Mama's room and explained it to her the best way I could. I had never even heard the word rape, so I didn't know that's what had happened to me.

As I tried to explain everything to Mama, I remembered a phone call between her and Aunt Sammie Joe about the stain on my aunt's green Victorian sofa. *My* stain. We had the same furniture in our living room, but the upholstery was a lighter, flowered pattern. At the time I overheard the conversation, my aunt couldn't figure out what it was, and if they ever connected the dots, they didn't say so.

I didn't want to relive that horrible incident, and after my mother spoke to a lawyer, it was decided that we would not press charges against Phillip, primarily to protect me from the harshness and scrutiny of a trial. When my brother Don, who was an adult with a child of his own by then, found out I was pregnant, he asked how he could make it better. Eventually, I told him what happened and he went looking for Phillip. Mama and Aunt Sammie Joe talked Don out of hurting Phillip, or worse. My cousin Charles was just as angry and never had anything to do with Phillip again.

When I told Bonita that I was pregnant, she told me that their mother suspected that Phillip had someone pregnant because he had been sick. (I found out years later that men sometimes experience morning sickness just like pregnant women do.) He denied it, of course. The news of my pregnancy spread from Bonita to her mother, then to her older sisters, and although Bonita stayed loyal to me, the others were quick to defend their brother. They accused me of lying on Phillip and even about being pregnant at all, and always said mean things to me. For the most part, I ignored them.

So here I was, just a few months after my 13th birthday, pregnant. I was going to have a baby. Many of the conversations about me didn't involve me, but Mama did present me with the option of ending the pregnancy. She wasn't necessarily advocating for it; she simply let me know it was an option. Well, that was never an option for me. I was going to keep this baby. Although I was too young and uninformed to completely understand everything, somehow I was sure about that.

Luckily, I didn't begin to really show until I was about six months pregnant, so I was able to finish the school year without incident. For those first few months, I dealt with the pregnancy mentally and emotionally, since there were no notable physical changes. Other than Bonita, I hadn't told anyone outside of my immediate family about my "condition." Once the school year ended, I was sent to live with one of my mother's cousins in Boston, Massachusetts, until I had the baby. Unbeknownst to me, the plan was for me to have the baby and leave it in Boston for our cousin to raise.

In Boston, I spent the weekdays at the Florence Crittenton Home for Unwed Mothers. It was a residential program that taught us life skills and our rights as parents. My case worker, Ruby Morton, took me shopping for maternity clothes. I also participated in counseling sessions to help me deal with this life-changing situation. One of the goals of counseling was to prevent me from blaming my baby for what had happened to me. I couldn't imagine how anything could be a baby's fault, but I listened and tried to understand. On the weekends, I took the bus or caught a ride back to my cousin's house. Strangely, I don't remember anyone being outraged by my pregnancy, and, outside of the home for unwed mothers, no one really talked about the situation at all. I guess the silence was the result of people not knowing what to say to a 13-year-old pregnant rape victim.

Our cousin was very religious and sometimes had ministers visit her home to pray and teach about the Bible. On one such visit, the minister addressed me. "You're going to have a boy," he told me. I tuned him out almost immediately. However, I knew better than to say anything disrespectful, so I didn't interrupt him, and he kept talking. "His name will begin with an 'M' and he will be a man of God."

Whatever, I thought. My cousin was moved by his prophecy, but I wasn't. I wanted a girl, and had already chosen a name for her. Nothing this minister said was going to change that.

9

That September, I celebrated my 14th birthday with family at my cousin's house in Boston. Around this time, I became aware of changes in my body. I was seven months pregnant and took my growing belly in stride since everyone in the home for unwed mothers looked just like me. Shockingly, I was not the youngest resident at the home; an 11-year-old was also there. There were also some young adults present, like the 21-year-old who was pregnant from a married politician in her town. Although she was of age, the scandal would have ruined her life and his career, so she was sent away to have the baby.

One night at the residential home, I woke up to go to the bathroom. By the time I got there, I didn't have to go anymore. I returned to the room I shared, but soon after lying down, I felt like I had to go again. All of this movement awakened my roommate. When I explained to her what was going on, she called the house mother. After a few questions, the house mother concluded that I was having contractions.

That is when the panic set in. It was happening. It was really happening! I was having a baby, and all of the "normalcy" I had mentally created about the situation slipped away. Any feelings I had buried came bursting to the top. I had put so much of my time and mental energy into understanding what would happen when it was time for the baby to come, and now it was happening. For the first time, I cried. I cried because I was scared. I cried because things were happening that I could not control and I just didn't know what to do. I cried because, despite all of the information I had been taught over the past few months, I was overwhelmed by the enormity of this responsibility.

The house mother called the hospital and tried unsuccessfully to calm me down. The family I had been raised with was over a thousand miles away; I was surrounded by people but felt completely alone. I was taken to the hospital by ambulance, and after seven hours of labor, my son was born on November 18, 1975. One of my cousins was a nurse at the hospital, so although I don't remember who, if anyone, rode to the hospital in the ambulance with me, I do remember that my cousin Bell was there when my baby was born. I named him Maurice

Alexander McBride. My tears had stopped by then, and many of the details are a blur, but when I held my son in my arms, it became clear to me what I had to do. It didn't matter how he had been conceived. It didn't matter how young I was. It didn't matter what people thought or said. When the hospital nurse handed me my bundle, all that mattered was that I had a responsibility. I now had someone depending on me, and at that moment, although I was still overwhelmed by everything that had transpired in the last few months, I knew what I had to do. I had to secure a future for my son and myself, and the only way I knew to do that was through education. That moment reaffirmed my commitment to getting as much education as I could to make sure that Maurice was well taken care of.

I remained in Boston for two weeks after giving birth, then I brought Maurice home for my mama to see. Soon after I arrived, a social worker visited the house. She explained that she was there to place Maurice in a foster home until we could keep him at our home. I didn't understand why we couldn't keep him right then, but it was still 1975 and I was still a child in my mother's house. This was my baby, but I felt powerless in this decision-making process.

The social worker, my mother, and I took Maurice to Louisville, Georgia, where he lived with a foster family for four months. I didn't understand why he was there, but I made sure Mama took me to see him every weekend so I could bond with him, because I fully expected to get him back. On the social worker's next and final visit, she brought up adoption.

"I hadn't planned to put him up for adoption," I told her. I remembered what my mama had told me about adoption a few years earlier. Not only was I adopted, my cousin Charles was, too. Mama and Aunt Sammie Joe had adopted us around the same time. Based on the good lives Charles and I lived, I knew that adoption could be a positive thing, but in the home for unwed mothers in Boston, I had been taught that I had options, no matter how young I was and no matter the circumstances. I was Maurice's mother and I knew the decision to keep him or put him up for adoption was mine.

The social worker was baffled. She addressed my mother. "Matt Lee, I thought he was being put up for adoption." My mother's only response was a look that seemed to say, "So did I." Well, Maurice was my son and this was my decision. I chose to keep him. There was never any question in my mind or heart about this. At 14, I didn't know much about parenting, but I knew I wanted my baby and I knew I had a right to keep him. I didn't care about how he had been conceived; he was my baby and I loved him.

"Well, I guess we're keeping him," Mama said. And that was the end of that. The social worker left, and a day or two later, we drove to Louisville to get my son after buying a crib and other necessities. I'm guessing that at some point my mother let her cousin in Boston know that she would not be raising my son as her own. No one ever talked to me about it. I suppose my resolve to keep Maurice had put an end to that conversation before it began.

And now, here I sit, almost 38 years later, watching Maurice cross the stage to receive his doctorate. No one predicted that the child who had been born to a child, who had so many behavior problems, who dropped out of high school to pursue a rap career, who had spent years having brushes with the law, and who had been incarcerated for repeated violations would be sharing this platform with his young mother. Ours is an amazing story that includes fun, laughter, and love, shaped by strife, hurt, and confusion. Yet, it is ours. We claim it, we own it, and now we share it with the world.

Chapter 2
The New Kid

Maurice

"Dr. Vickie McBride."

I place my degree cover beside me so that I can applaud for my mother. As I watch this petite woman cross the same stage I had crossed just minutes earlier, wearing the same doctoral regalia that I sported, I think about all that she went through - all that *we* went through - to get here. This is a moment I will never forget. "That's my mama!" I yell. She smiles and holds back tears as she's hooded and shakes hands with Mr. McKinney, the president of Capella University. As she continues to shake hands with everyone before exiting the stage, memories of our lives flood my brain... I'm four years old, sitting on her stomach as she lay in bed, listening to me explain why I ripped all of Mrs. Opeil's flowers from her garden... I'm seven years old, riding a bus by myself after a weekend visit with Vickie when she was a student at Savannah State College, crying because I always hated to leave her and missed her before I even made it back to my grandmother in Waynesboro, Georgia... I'm eight years old, and after years of begging, Vickie has finally given me a baby brother named Jon. I love him immediately and deeply. Life with Vickie was wonderful in those early years.

And then there are the memories that aren't so wonderful. I can't stop my mind from dredging up the painful images that push their way into my consciousness... The infuriated yelling, the severe beatings I endured at Vickie's hand when I did something wrong, the physical confrontations that began when I thought I was fighting for my life... If it hadn't been for Mattie Lee McBride, a respected teacher who adopted my mother and retired from her career to raise me while my mother went to high school, I would not have survived. Although I knew who my mother was, my grandmother was "Mama" and my mother was "Vickie." I was a grown man before I knew it bothered Vickie that I addressed her

13

by her name. I now affectionately call her "mother dear." She is, in fact, dear to me. I loved her then, and I love her now, but I wouldn't have made it to this historic moment - a mother and child earning doctorates from the same school on the same day - without the love of my mama.

After Vickie graduated from high school and went away to college, I stayed with Mama and spent summers with Vickie. This living arrangement continued even after Vickie graduated from Savannah State College. When my fourth grade school year ended, Vickie arrived in Waynesboro with my baby brother in tow. She had been married and was separated by then, and was still living in Savannah, Georgia. We put my belongings in her car and headed back there. As always, I was excited about going to live with them. My early memories of our time together were some of my best, and visits with Vickie had always been great. We went to cool places, did new and exciting things, ate lots of good food, and always had fun. I imagined that my life with Vickie and Jon would be wonderful. But things took a turn for the worse almost immediately.

The three of us lived in a townhome. My brother and I shared an upstairs bedroom to the left of the staircase. We had twin beds, the floor was tile, and the window was covered with cheap blinds - a far cry from Mama's brick house with Victorian furniture in the formal living room, two china cabinets in the formal dining room, custom linen on every bed, and custom blinds and drapes throughout the house. I didn't care one bit. I was happy to be with Vickie and Jon.

When Vickie went to work, I was given strict instructions not to let anyone into the house. I promised I would not. Since my brother was in daycare, I was home alone and decided to go outside. It was hard being the new kid, but I wasn't afraid to make new friends. After meeting a few people and playing for a while, I went back inside.

A short while later, there was a knock at the door. One of the boys I had met asked if he could come in for a drink of water. I knew I wasn't supposed to let him in, but I wanted to make friends, so I didn't say no. After a couple of minutes, there was another knock at the door. A friend of his wanted to come in. I said yes again. After a few more knocks at the door, there were about eight boys from the neighborhood in Vickie's house. I knew they needed to leave, but I didn't know how to tell them to go. While I was trying to figure it out, one of them asked me to help him look for a pen he had lost somewhere in our apartment. I didn't understand how he could have lost anything, but I helped him look anyway. We didn't find it. By the time we made it back to the living room, everybody was in a hurry to leave, and I was relieved.

I spent the rest of the day waiting for Vickie and Jon to come back home. When Vickie came through the door with my brother on her hip, she was furious. "Who's been in my motherfucking house?" she screamed at me. "I told you not to let anyone in!" I could feel the waves of anger rolling off of her.

"Nobody," I lied.

"Nobody, huh? Then why did some little bastards outside just try to sell me my own stuff? They have my checkbook, credit cards, jewelry… Why the hell did you let their bad asses in here?" I was too scared and confused to do anything but deny it, but she knew better. She went upstairs and changed from her work clothes to a t-shirt, sweatpants, and sneakers. "I'ma beat your ass when I get back," she promised, and went outside to confront the boys and get her stuff back.

I took my brother upstairs to our room. I had been played - taken advantage of. Nothing like this had ever happened to me before. I had done some bad things by that point in my life - stealing, lying, fighting - but I had never been on the receiving end of it. Worse, I felt guilty for doing something that had hurt Vickie. I loved her. The shame and guilt were overwhelming, and I cried. Jon sat on my bed next to me, held my hand, and tried to soothe me, but I was inconsolable in my disgrace and fear. Crystal came over that day and found me in the bedroom in tears. She was one of my mother's friends who was often at our house. After I explained what happened, she was sympathetic and tried to calm me down, but she could not assuage my guilt, and the tears kept flowing. Vickie had been violated, and it was all my fault. I

15

deserved punishment, but like any child, I didn't want it, so I tried to think of a way to make it better. Nothing came to me.

I could hear Vickie outside yelling at the boys as she tried to reclaim her belongings. "Bad asses... You little bastards better give me all of my shit!" Her verbal tirade continued. She was hurt and she was *mad*. I still wasn't ready for what I heard her say next. "Y'all come on to the house and watch Maurice get this ass whooping."

What?

"Come on, 'cause I'm about to beat his ass!"

In that moment, I knew she was serious, and I knew I couldn't let that happen. I was the new kid and these boys had already taken advantage of me. I couldn't let her make it worse by publicly humiliating me.

Vickie kept her promise. "Bring your ass down here!" she screamed up the stairs from the living room. "Since you want to show off for these bastards, I'ma show them you getting your ass beat." Crystal tried to calm Vickie down when she came back into the house, but it was going to take more than reasoning to curb her anger.

"No!" I yelled back. Those boys could not witness my punishment. It would be over for me. "I'm not coming down there," I screamed through my tears. I didn't want to disobey, but this was too much.

Black belt in hand, Vickie came upstairs and gave me the worst beating I had ever experienced. Every lick was accompanied by a verbal blow as she attempted to drag me downstairs for public humiliation, but I wasn't going. *I couldn't.* I held on to anything I could grab - the bed, the door, the rail - but she was relentless; angrier than I'd ever seen her. She was *enraged*. And strong. She dragged me down the stairs, adding knots and bruises to the sting of the belt and the stab of her words.

Crystal had taken Jon from the room, and by the time my mother forced me down the stairs into the living room, all four of us were crying. I was still trying to escape the embarrassment of an audience, grabbing onto the coffee table in the living room as she dragged me to the kitchen where I could see a large group of boys standing outside of the sliding glass door, watching. The lash of the belt was intensified as I became aware of the spectators, and then I slipped and fell in the blood on the tile.

Blood.

My blood. The nosebleed that had started somewhere on the staircase made the floor slippery and made me believe I was dying. Vickie was trying to kill me, I thought, and I didn't want to die. Somehow, I got on my feet and started fighting back. Before I saw the blood, I had only been trying to block the blow of the belt and escape, but now I was swinging. At that age, I was still a little shorter than Vickie, and I wasn't trying to hurt her. In my mind, I was trying to survive. I fought to stay on my feet. I couldn't fall again because if I went down, I would never get back up. I would die in the bright red smear of my blood on the tile.

My first swing landed and stunned both of us, but after a startled second, I realized that fighting back only infuriated Vickie more. So we wrestled. Crystal kept screaming for her to stop, but the yelling, cursing, fighting, and crying continued. Crystal ran to the sliding glass door and let down the blinds, but they were too short to reach all the way to the floor. *Boom!* I will never forget the sound of those kids dropping to the ground in unison to witness this unnatural battle.

Somehow, Crystal's tearful pleading penetrated the haze of my mother's fury and she stopped. She was tired, she was hurt, and she was weeping. I didn't know what to do. I was sent to my room, and I sat in there alone with my feelings of shame, humiliation, fear, and regret. I had hurt Vickie. Because of me, she had been violated and victimized. Worse, I had *hit* her. I was wrong, but I didn't believe that I'd had a choice. Still, I was ashamed.

The rest of that day is a blur. I don't remember dinner or getting ready for bed, but I do remember the reaction of the neighborhood boys when I went outside the next day. Strangely, they were impressed. "Man, you crazy!" they said. Children didn't hit their parents, and since I had done just that, they were in awe of me. I accepted their adulation, but I wasn't proud of what I had done.

Unfortunately, this would not be the last time something of this nature happened between Vickie and me. The story ends well, of course, but it is not a completely happy story to tell. It reflects a life wrought with pain and abandonment, punctuated with brief periods of happiness. It is a story of love and forgiveness. It is my story. It is her story. It is our true story.

Chapter 3
A Girl Who Would

Vickie

I spent all four years of high school as a parent. I started ninth grade while at the Florence Crittenton Home for Unwed Mothers in Boston, so when I returned home to Waynesboro, Georgia, I enrolled at the local high school and continued my education. My mother had earned a bachelor's degree from Savannah State College, and up until the time she retired to care for Maurice so that I could attend high school, she was an elementary school teacher. Education was important in our family, and having a baby didn't change that for me. My mother always said, "Baby, if you want to be able to provide for your children the way I have provided for you, you have to do what I did." So I planned to go to college just as she had done.

I was raised in a brick house on a corner lot on Doyle Street, which was later re-named Martin Luther King Jr. Drive. The front of the house faces the projects directly across the street, and a segregated cemetery is across Blakeney Street to the right. Mama had a green thumb, so our yard, especially the back yard, was picturesque when the trees and flowers bloomed. When I was growing up, there was nothing to the left of the house or behind it, but eventually, a middle class neighborhood sprang up around us as more black families were able to afford new homes. My parents were well-known and highly respected in our town. My father, Thomas McBride, owned and operated a local funeral home. He was a powerful man; the local American Legion is named after him. He also formed the Burke County Citizens Development Corporation to improve employment opportunities for black citizens in the county. My mother was a shrewd business woman who came from a well-to-do family. In addition to helping my father run his funeral home, she also sold insurance. As a result of their hard work and wise planning, I had everything I needed and got most of what I desired, and I wanted to provide the same lifestyle for Maurice, so foregoing my high school education for a low-paying job was *never* an option.

I loved being a mommy! The way I became a parent was terrible, but spending time with my son was wonderful. My mother loved me unconditionally, but she was the type of woman who showed her love by buying things. There was very little affection and rarely an "I love you." I took a different approach with Maurice; I was all over him. I held him all the time and showered him with kisses. In fact, I was very loving and affectionate with all of my children, but it began with my first son.

Although I dealt with the typical small town attitudes toward unmarried teenage mothers, I didn't hide Maurice and often took him with me to school events like football and basketball games, and pep rallies when he got old enough. Though my body showed no signs of having had a baby, I never denied him, nor did I try to pass him off as my brother. Mama, on the other hand, thought differently. When we were in public shortly after I brought Maurice home from Louisville for good, people would ask me, "Is this your baby?" Before I could respond, Mama would say, "That's *my* baby." I got the message. Since no one had actually seen me pregnant, it might have been easy to deny that I had a child, but I didn't see the need. I felt no shame about having a baby because I knew I had done nothing wrong. Still, when someone asked me that question, I took my cue from Mama and usually chose not to respond at all.

Some people who didn't know what really happened assumed I was "fast" and said horrible things about me, and Phillip's sisters were relentless in their attacks on me in defense of their brother. I could tongue wrestle with the best of them, and although I never heard such words at home, I learned to curse and was good at it, so I didn't back down from people's oral assaults. Sometimes the taunts got so bad that I responded to the verbal bullying from other kids with my fists, and that got me into trouble. If an argument started, it usually wasn't long before I beat somebody down when he or she didn't heed my warning to stop, and my mother found out about it every single time, but I didn't care. My power had been taken away once, and it wasn't going to happen again.

The one thing that did hurt, however, was that I lost a couple of good friends because their mothers told them not to hang around "girls like me." I was also very disappointed when I practiced and tried out for the cheerleading squad so that I could remain active during basketball season when marching band was over, but wasn't selected because a school committee didn't think my presence on the squad would set a "good example" for other girls. I carried the pain of this misjudgment with me for many years, but eventually accepted that, wrong as they were, those adults were doing the best they could at that time to guide children in the right direction. I've long since forgiven them.

Still, I went to school, participated in other extracurricular activities, like band, and did things that typical high school students did, like go to the prom and work part time. One job was at the local Dairy Queen, and when I got my first check, which was about $50, I was super excited! One of the first things I did was take Maurice to Benbrook's Five & Dime to have pictures taken. I also did other teenage things, like invite my friends over when Mama wasn't home. Our house had an intercom system; I would blast music through it and my friends and I would snap our fingers and dance around the living room. Maurice would try to join us, but he could barely walk, let alone dance, and he couldn't snap his fingers at all, but it was funny to watch him try.

The one thing I didn't do was "mess with boys." Since my first and only experience with a boy had been so horrible, I was scared that all experiences would be the same way and have the same result. I loved Maurice, but there was no way I wanted to go through any of that again. That didn't stop boys or grown men from approaching me. One such man was a 28-year-old that caught my attention. I was young, but I had a baby and thought that meant I was mature enough to at least handle talking to him. Mama was livid!

"Who are his people?" she inquired. She asked this same question about every friend I had or boy I talked to. Things like family name and reputation were very important to Mrs. Mattie

21

Lee McBride, but I couldn't have cared less. When I misbehaved or did anything that wasn't acceptable, she would say, "That kind of thing isn't expected of a McBride."

"And?" I retorted each time, with as much flippant disregard as I dared. My teenage rebellion was in full swing, and I pushed any limits that were based on what people might think.

Mama forbade me to see this grown man, but I disobeyed and visited him at his mother's house anyway. Strangely, his family didn't balk at the idea of a man who was closer to 30 than 20 entertaining a 14-year-old. He never tried to have sex with me, and after talking for a few weeks, he left me alone. I guess he realized how inappropriate a relationship with me would be.

I had my first boyfriend in the 11th grade. By now, most of my friends were developing the hips, butt, and breasts I'd had for over three years. We were at an age where the opposite gender was often the topic of conversation, but I didn't have the same giddy anticipation about sex that most of them had. My boyfriend was from a neighboring city that bussed their students to our high school. I usually didn't date boys from my small town, preferring the ones who lived in surrounding cities so that I wouldn't have to deal with them every day. I guess I had commitment issues even then. My boyfriend and I had fun together, but I was very uncomfortable anytime we were alone. By then, of course, I knew that sex made babies, so I didn't want to have sex. Soon after we began dating, I explained how I became a parent and told my boyfriend that I understood completely if he wanted to break up so that he could find a girlfriend that would have sex with him because I simply couldn't do it. He was very understanding and said he was okay not having sex. He left me about six months later for a girl who would.

At some point that year, Phillip, Maurice's father, showed up at my door. He was either heading to the military or just returning home for a visit. I wasn't afraid when I saw him. I had determined long ago that if he ever tried to hurt me again, he would regret it. After saying hello, Phillip said, "I wanna see the baby you say is mine." I was shocked that he was still acting like paternity was a question, but I guess I shouldn't have been.

I didn't invite him in, but I agreed to let him see Maurice, who was about two at the time, and strongly favored his father's side of the family. Maurice came to me when I called him. Phillip stared, but didn't speak. After a few seconds, Maurice wobbled away.

Phillip looked at me. "Can we get together again?" he asked.

What? I thought. *Is he serious?*

"We need to get together again and raise him," he continued.

Again? Did he think we had "gotten together" the first time? I stared at him incredulously. I could see right through his game. He didn't want a relationship with me, he wanted sex. I was seething and ready to fight, and this time I wouldn't lose.

"Hell no!" I told him. "You knew he was yours and denied it all of this time. Now you want to act like you're just finding out?"

"You never told me you were pregnant," Phillip said. "I didn't know he was mine, and you never made me take responsibility."

"But you knew because Bonita told you, and you and my cousin Charles were good friends," I countered. "And you're right, I didn't make you take responsibility, and I won't. I've never asked you for anything and I never will!" I continued before he could speak. "Besides, I'm going to college. I'm not hanging around here to be with you or anyone else." If he said something else after that, I don't remember it. He left my porch and never approached me like that again.

I continued to date, but I didn't have a serious relationship until the summer before my senior year of high school. I went to T. W. Josey High School in Augusta about 30 minutes away to earn a credit I needed to be a senior since no summer classes were offered at Waynesboro High School. There, I met an amazing boy named Tommy. Not only was he incredibly fine, but he played the guitar and had a different quality about him that really attracted me. He felt the same way about me, and our relationship was my first summer love. Surprisingly, I was okay emotionally, mentally, and physically. I didn't have flashbacks, and I was able to enjoy being with a man for the first time. We would spend our afternoons together when school ended, and we talked on the phone all the time. He never came to Waynesboro, and never even knew that I had a child. While at Crittenton in Boston, I had been taught about and prescribed birth control pills, so there was no danger of me getting pregnant. Even though I wasn't a virgin, it was my first time consenting and my first time enjoying sex. When the summer ended, our relationship did, too, except for a few phone calls. I was okay with that.

During my senior year, I had another boyfriend. I offered him the same explanation I had offered the boy before Tommy, and the same exit option. Even though I'd had sex with Tommy and I knew that sex was important to boys, I still wasn't ready to allow it to be an expected part of every relationship I had. Like my junior year boyfriend, this one treated me well and didn't pressure me. He hung in there as long as he could, but after a year or so, he also left me for a girl who would have sex.

After graduating from Waynesboro High School, I went off to college at age 17. My mama's friends had warned her that educating me was a waste of time and money because I wasn't going to do anything but have a house full of babies. In her infinite wisdom, she ignored them, and we planned my educational future. I was looking forward to getting away from home, but I was bothered about being away from Maurice. He was my partner; I took him everywhere with me, except on dates. I was going to miss him dearly. I don't know if he understood that I was leaving or not.

Heeding my mother's advice about needing a good education to provide for myself and my child, I had planned to attend Clark University in Atlanta, Georgia, with some friends, but we had a big falling out the summer before our freshman year, so my mother sent me to Georgia Southern College in Statesboro instead. I used financial aid, grants, and assistance for single mothers to pay for school. I never hid the fact that I had a child, and the news didn't garner much of a reaction from students or staff at the college.

My first roommate was a white girl named Judy Bradford. She was from another state, and we shared a room in Winburn Hall at GSC. In the beginning she was okay, but things turned sour very quickly. With so many years between my brother and me, I had practically been raised as an only child. I was not in the habit of sharing my clothes or other possessions. My mama had worked too hard to give me what I needed and wanted, and it was not to be shared. My roommate thought differently. Although I told her "no" when she asked to wear my clothes, whenever I wasn't around, she ignored what I told her and dressed from my closet anyway. I warned her repeatedly to stop. One time, she even took the comforter off of my bed to sit on at an outside event. I thought to myself, *So the one* your *mama bought is too good to throw on the ground, but the one* my *mama bought is trash?* That was it! She completely disregarded my verbal requests to respect my personal boundaries, so I decided to speak the universal language of whoop-ass that I was sure she would understand.

On my way to find her, I made sure I let the Resident Assistant and everyone else in the dormitory know that I was looking for her and why. The RA tried, but she couldn't talk me out of beating some sense into Judy. By the time Judy came back to our room, she knew I was looking for her and why. She got a few words out before I started getting licks in. She ended up with cuts and bruises, and I ended up with a disciplinary record. Needless to say, she was the only dormitory roommate I ever had.

I don't remember much else about my freshman year. I had so much fun that most of it is a blur of parties, parties, and more parties. I went to class sometimes. I think. Mostly, I spent my time finding out which fraternities were having parties, getting ready to go to parties, and having fun at parties. Since I was an Omega Psi Phi Sweetheart, I felt that my presence at all Que parties was mandatory. I attended some of the other fraternities' parties, too. Why discriminate? I can honestly say that I loved "attending" Georgia Southern College, the glaring truth of which is reflected on my transcript.

I met my first college friends, Sharmaine and Alucia, at GSC. Sharmaine was from Atlanta, and we clicked instantly. We were the same age and our birthdays were close. We did a lot together then, and are still the best of friends now. One major difference between us is that Sharmaine was a serious student. She was taking advanced courses while I was taking remedial ones. The summer following our freshman year, I went to summer school and got out of remedial classes. I had never been a straight 'A' student, but there was no way I was going to remain in remedial classes. Sharmaine influenced me to do better, and I actually earned credits my sophomore year. Alucia was from Savannah, Georgia, and we are also still close. The three of us had loads of fun together (the details of which are withheld to protect the not-so-innocent), but we made sure that we were passing our classes, too. I didn't have any problems with these two like the ones I'd had with Judy.

During the week, I had a great time in college. Since GSC was only about an hour away from my hometown, I could visit Mama and Maurice on the weekends. I always looked forward to seeing my son on these visits, but the quality time I planned to spend with him quickly turned into a time for disciplining him.

Mama, who was now close to 70 years old, was no match for the spoiled, defiant preschooler without any boundaries, which is what Maurice had become. She would call me almost every day while I was at GSC to tell me that Maurice had done something wrong and that I would have to punish him when I got there that weekend. You can imagine how ineffective weekend disciplining was for a four-year-old. What good was it to punish a child on Saturday for something he had done on Monday or Tuesday? Too much time had passed for the lesson to be meaningful.

While I had lived in her house, Mama had punished me for misbehavior and had done everything she could to ensure that I walked a straight line. Up until I was about 10, I got whippings as punishment, sometimes administered by my older brother, but after I got my period, I was grounded when I broke the rules instead. Once I had Maurice, however, Mama and I were constantly at odds over how to raise him. Since she raised both of us and Maurice also called her "Mama," she didn't really acknowledge that I was his mother, and that, even as a teenager, I had my own views on parenting. Although she punished him occasionally, her parenting style with Maurice was tolerant and indulgent; mine was structured and had rewards for good behavior and punishment for bad behavior. Needless to say, Maurice gravitated toward Mama's brand of parenting. Her basic belief was that if I couldn't pay the bills in her house, I couldn't say anything. This created a rift in my relationship with Mama that lasted until shortly before she died.

I managed to have a boyfriend, Jermaine, my freshman year of college. I shared my story with him as I had the others, and he was patient. He didn't pressure me about sex, and after being with Jermaine for a little over a year, I felt ready to have a physical relationship again. Jermaine was understanding and very thoughtful, so all aspects of my relationship with him were pleasurable. But I had to let him go when Maurice became very ill and I saw who Jermaine really was.

One day, I came home from class and my Uncle Alexander was in my dorm room. This couldn't be good.

"Hey. What are you doing here?" I asked.

"Pack your things, Vickie. You need to come with me," my uncle said.

"Where are we going? Why can't I drive?" My first car was a 1970-something Buick. Instead of using that car to go on road trips with my college friends, I used it to come home almost every weekend because of Maurice's behavior.

Uncle Alexander repeated what he had already said in response. I couldn't drive my own car, and I couldn't ask questions until we were in his car and on the way to Waynesboro. A few minutes into the trip, I asked, "What has he done now?" I knew this had to be about Maurice.

"Maurice is in the hospital. He's real sick. I can't go into detail. Let your mother explain at the hospital," he said. We rode in silence the rest of the way home. *The hospital?* By now, I was feeling anxious and the lack of answers only made it worse. This wasn't a head cold or a scraped knee. My baby was sick enough to be in the hospital. My anxiety grew with each passing mile.

When we arrived at the Burke County Hospital, Maurice was asleep in the hospital bed with Mama by his side. When I approached her, she wailed, "Oh, Lord, my baby almost died!" When she could pull herself together, she explained that Maurice had been complaining about his head hurting, kept stumbling when he tried to walk, and kept refusing to go to bed. He was also burning with fever. When she took him to his pediatrician, Dr. Shelley Griffin, the next morning, he was having trouble breathing. Dr. Griffin did a spinal tap and Maurice screamed in pain but was too weak to move. When Dr. Griffin saw that the fluid from the spinal tap was cloudy, he diagnosed Maurice with viral meningitis, scooped him up in his arms, and rushed him to the hospital. He told Mama that, had she taken him to the hospital in Augusta the night before, the shot they would have given him to reduce the fever would have killed him. She was inconsolable at the thought that she could have been responsible for Maurice's death.

When I was nine or 10 years old, a girl that I used to walk to school with had died of meningitis, but hers had been bacterial whereas Maurice's was viral. The doctor explained that, because of this difference, it was likely that Maurice would survive. Still, Mama called in the heavy artillery. She was a huge Oral Roberts fan and sometimes donated to his church. Mama called them and Oral's son, Richard Roberts, came to pray for Maurice. I was a bundle of emotions. I didn't know if his prayer would be any more effective than ours, but I was willing to give anything a try. There was really nothing I could do, but I stayed by Maurice's bedside for a week anyway. I cried, I worried, and I prayed. Why *my* baby? What could I have done to prevent this? I pleaded with God to heal him.

Mama visited every day, and Dr. Griffin checked on Maurice regularly. My boyfriend, Jermaine, came to visit, and it was then that I realized he either didn't like kids or just didn't like *my* kid. He never asked about Maurice at all; he just kept trying to make me come back to school. When I tried to explain that my baby was sick and I had to stay, he said, "I don't know what the big deal is." That is when I knew the relationship was over. Any man who couldn't understand a mother's concern for her child who was fighting a potentially fatal illness was not one I could have in my life. I had to let him go.

I went to campus one weekend to get some of my things and came back to Waynesboro the following week. Maurice had improved, thank God, and instead of sleeping days away in a hospital bed, he was running around in the Batman underoos I had bought him, making friends with everyone in the hospital. Just before he was about to be released, he was diagnosed with chicken pox! Apparently, he had caught them from one of his new hospitalized friends. He spent another week there, and this time, he couldn't visit anyone. I wasn't that worried about the chicken pox. My son had made it through the life-threatening illness, so I started going back to campus more frequently.

During one of my trips back to GSC, Dr. Griffin said that Maurice could be discharged. Mama dressed him in the striped shirt and jeans with the patched knee that he had come to the hospital in, and took him home. I called regularly to check on him and could tell he was back to his normal self. I felt a huge sense of relief knowing that my son was going to be okay. Jermaine was still trying to beg his way back into my life, but there was no way I would have a relationship with a man who didn't care about my son and couldn't understand why I did. I didn't know it then, but this wouldn't be the last time Maurice affected my relationship with a man. For the next 11 years, my son would have an effect on my relationships in ways I simply could not have imagined.

Chapter 4
Kiss My Booty!

Maurice

Despite the trauma I experienced when I got older, my early childhood with Mama and Vickie was great. I lived in a home with two women who loved me, and I didn't want for anything. As an adult, I realized that I had been spoiled. Mama's family had been well-off, and she and my grandfather had prospered when he owned a funeral home. Although Mama punished me when I misbehaved, she could afford to indulge my every desire, sometimes against Vickie's wishes. I didn't have any chores or responsibilities, which was a major point of contention between the two of them. As I said, I knew that Vickie was my mother, but during those early years, we were like siblings. Mama was raising both of us.

Before I was old enough to go to school, a friend would occasionally get dropped off at my house and I would have a playmate for the day. For the most part, however, I spent my days with Mama and her friends, watching TV and playing with my toys while Vickie was in high school. I was around for many of the conversations these elderly women had, but never took part in them unless I was addressed directly. Mama was as old school as they come, so children were still seen and not heard. She was also unwavering about "correcting" my left-handedness, and it was practically a crime to wash clothes or do anything but the Lord's work on a Sunday.

I started attending daycare at age four. Mama drove me there on the first day, but after that, I caught the bus. When I returned home each day, Mama always had a snack waiting for me. We would sit at the table and eat together and talk. Those times are some of my fondest memories.

My first interaction with kids from the projects was at daycare. I got quite an education at that place, and most of it had nothing to do with the curriculum (if there was one). One day, I was using the restroom and a girl named Gia came in and pulled her pants down. Since my pants were already down, I just stood there, not knowing what to say or do. The look on my face must have told her that I needed instructions. "Put that here," Gia said, pointing at me and then at herself. I didn't know what she was talking about, but I could tell it was something I wasn't supposed to be doing. Besides, Mama had told me not to let anyone touch my "privates" or everything would fall off. It looked like Gia's had already fallen off, so I pulled up my pants and got out of that bathroom quick!

Another memorable incident occurred during nap time. For some reason, a girl named Alisha decided to kiss each boy's butt that came to her cot. I don't remember how it got started - it may have been a dare - but I do remember giggling as I watched Alisha lay patiently on her cot and wait as boy after boy jumped up from his cot, ran to hers, pulled down his pants, and got a nice little peck on his naked butt cheeks. The room erupted in suppressed giggles each time she did it, sending the boy with the freshly-smooched bottom scurrying back to his assigned space.

"Kiss *my* booty!" another boy would challenge.

"Come on," Alisha would say, and the boy would be up and on his way to her cot amid whispered laughter and tiny-toothed grins. I was laughing so hard I could barely get up when I heard my name.

"It's your turn, Maurice! Go! Hurry up!" the kids whispered. Finally, it was my turn to get my booty kissed! I jumped up, ran to Alisha's cot, pulled down my pants and underwear, and squatted, anticipating the peck that would send me running back to my cot before the adults saw me. I smiled at my friend, Demond, who had already joined the Alisha-kissed-my-booty club, and waited for the smack that would make me a member. She didn't move.

"Come on, girl, hurry up before they come in!" I squatted a little lower to make sure she could reach it. Still, Alisha didn't move. What was she waiting on? Then I noticed how quiet it was. No whispering. No giggling.

"Maurice, what are you doing?" I heard an adult voice say. "Why are your pants down? Come here!" My smile disappeared as I snatched up my clothes and did as I was told. It was just my luck that I was the one who got caught. The real problem was that I couldn't explain what I was doing or why. How does a four-year-old tell an adult about a booty-kissing game? I didn't fully understand it myself; I just knew I wanted my booty kissed because the other boys did it. God only knows what Alisha thought she was doing or why she thought it was okay. At that point, none of that mattered. I was punished, and that's all I cared about.

The daycare was an uncaring place. We were punished instead of disciplined, and it was harsh. Once, an adult twisted my ear until it bled. The whole experience was like the movie *Training Day* for me. Adults ridiculed me for my mistakes, and sometimes pitted us against each other for their entertainment. Daycare is where I learned to fight. Often, the boys were lined up facing each other in front of the building, and when one of the adults said "Go!", we had to fight whoever was across from us. I lost the first two times this happened, and that's when I learned that I didn't like being defeated. After that, I never lost again.

I also remember that there was always competition for a toy car on a string. It was the one thing all of the boys wanted to play with. During playtime, whoever got it first had to fight to keep it. By the time I got the toy first, I had to fight *two* boys to keep it, and I did. The adults were impressed. That was my life as an only child - an outsider who didn't live in the projects and had no siblings or even cousins to fight with me or for me.

I know that Mama and Vickie had no idea what was happening to me in that place, just as the parents of the other children had no idea of the harm that was being done. I don't know why I never told anyone; I guess it doesn't occur to some children to tell things they are not asked. Honestly, I don't know what would have happened if Vickie had found out what was going on. She was a fighter, and I can only imagine the verbal and physical beatdown the adults would have endured. If I had put Vickie across from them and said "Go!", they wouldn't have had a chance.

But I didn't tell. Instead, I fought and I *survived*. As I've listened to other people's stories of mistreatment as small children over the years, I thank God that the experience wasn't much worse. I developed friendships in that heartless place, and a couple of them have lasted to this day. Demond and I still talk, and he remembers getting his booty kissed. It's still hilarious to us.

I also developed some other things, too, like the use of bad language, defiant behaviors, and the tendency to settle problems with physical confrontation. Those habits didn't serve me well and led to bigger problems later in life. Still, I had fun. There were some good times in daycare. We would skip around in a circle to the song, "Skip to My Lou," and we sometimes went on picnics at Magnolia Springs Park in Millen, a small city just a few miles away. Those were the times that made me look forward to going to kindergarten. Since Mama was a retired teacher, I knew that school would be the place where I would do more fun things like this, see my friends and meet new ones, play, and have a pretty good lunch. What child wouldn't look forward to that?

Despite these early experiences, I have always been a dreamer. I'm not sure where the tendency comes from, because I was raised by a very practical woman. Yet, I dream, and I dream big. The difference between me and most people is that I don't remain asleep. I wake up and make my dreams come true.

My earliest memory of dreaming about what I wanted to be was at age four. I wanted to be Elvis Presley. I loved the audience's reaction to him. Whenever he sang, or even when he just appeared on stage, everyone screamed and cheered and cried. At four, I wanted that reaction from a crowd, so I needed to be Elvis. To get ready for the day when I would be the one on stage, I practiced using an old volleyball pole at my great-aunt Sammie Joe's house as my microphone, and her dog Jo-Jo as my audience. I did this every time Mama and I visited her. My signature song was "Hound Dog," and I sang and danced my way through that song over and over again. Jo-Jo died after a few concerts. I hope it wasn't my singing that did it.

Once I heard Michael Jackson, the Elvis dream was over. I was seven years old and had to be Michael because he was cool.

The red jacket with studded shoulders, the shiny shoes and the glitter socks made him look smooth and invincible. Plus, he could spin around and not get dizzy! At seven, having this ability was a serious thing. Michael Jackson was doing what no one else could do, and I dreamed of being him. Mama bought me some things I needed, like the red jacket and some parachute pants, but I had to get the white glove on my own. She wouldn't buy one for me even though I begged her for one for the Christmas play at Waynesboro Elementary School. I had to wear a gray suit for the play, but I still needed that glove because, gray suit or not, I was going to be on stage, so I had to be Michael Jackson. Mama was either too old or not feeling well enough to come to the play, so she sent me with neighbors. Before leaving the house, I took one of her white church gloves from the top drawer of her chest and was the only child on stage playing the tambourine and representing Michael Jackson. The other kids loved it! I made sure I put the glove back when I got home, so Mama never knew I had taken it.

I started writing stories and drawing pictures at about the same age. I've always been creative, and that trait manifested in many different ways. I created my own board games, and even tried to make different foods, like peanut butter and jelly bologna sandwiches. There are still crayon marks on some of the bricks on the back of Mama's house from the time I tried to color it blue. I thought living in a blue house would be fun, but there were a lot of bricks, so I gave up after scribbling on a few.

The dream changed once again when I saw the group New Edition perform. I had heard their hit song "Candy Girl" on the radio, and when I saw them perform on TV, I was an instant fan. Not only was the audience going crazy, but the singers were kids like me! I still loved Michael Jackson, but after Vickie took me to see New Edition in concert, I knew what I had to do. I gathered up some of my friends and tried to make a singing group, but we were young and they couldn't see my vision, so every time we got together to practice, we ended up playing.

The official end of my Michael Jackson phase came when I was playing football in the back of Mrs. Latimore's house. A friend named Ra-Ra had a boombox, and that was the first time I heard the Fat Boys beatbox. I had never heard anything like that, and I immediately fell in love with beatboxing and rap. From the Fat Boys to LL Cool J to UTFO - I loved them all. At that time, rap music wasn't played on the radio like it is now, and the only time we could hear it was on Friday nights on a radio show called Fox Rocks. I asked my Mama for blank cassette tapes from Camelot, a record store in the mall, so I could record the show. A friend of mine had to show me how to record from the radio, but once I learned, it was on! I heard the Boogie Boys, Rapping Duke, Laid Back, Run DMC and many others. The kids in the neighborhood would have beatbox contests, and I practiced for hours on end until I was the best in the area.

Music was becoming the most important thing in my life. I wanted to rap and talk about rap all the time, even at school. I liked school, and getting good grades had never been a problem, but it wasn't long before I started feeling the pull of the streets even though I was still playing with transformers. I learned interesting things in school, but what I learned in the streets was way more captivating. Instead of hanging out in the neighborhood where my house was, I hung out in the projects across the street. Behind the projects, there was a gutted out abandoned building that we called The Hut. At about seven or eight o'clock each night, teens gathered at The Hut to hang out, play music, and dance. I was about ten years old and only in the fifth grade, but I loved music and could dance, so I had to be there.

I was hanging out at The Hut until the wee hours of the morning, and my aging mama was no match for me. When she found out I was misbehaving and could catch me, I knew I was in for it. The burn of the leather strap that she found every time I hid it, and the sting of the switches I kept having to break from the trees in the backyard are forever burned into my memory. Most of the time, I obeyed my mama, but when I disobeyed, I did things that she probably never imagined a child my age would do. She just couldn't handle me, and I took advantage of that.

Once, Mr. Terry, the father of a friend I played recreational baseball with, saw me in front of The Hut late at night. At that time, the whole village was raising the children, so Mr. Terry was one of the people who looked out for me. I usually rode to practice and to games with them since my mama couldn't drive me. He took me to my first professional baseball game when our rec team won the championship one year, and he was also the one who stopped his car when he saw me hanging out in front of The Hut.

"Maurice, come here!" he yelled from his window.

Uh oh. I walked over to Mr. Terry's car. "Yes, sir?"

"Boy, what are you doing out here? Do you know what time it is?"

"No," I said. That was the truth. I had no idea what time it was, but I knew it was late because there was a clock downtown that struck every hour. I'll never forget the adrenaline rush I felt each time I heard the deep chime because I was out when other kids my age were fast asleep.

"You don't belong out here with these bad boys. Get yo ass in this car, and if you let me catch you out here this time of night again, I'ma tear yo ass up! You hear me?"

"Yes, sir." I got in, knowing better than to try to argue. Mr. Terry took me home. On the way there, I got an earful.

"Don't let me catch you out here again," he told me on the short ride to my house. "You hear me? I'm not playing with you. Go in the house right now."

I went in, but the next night, I was back at The Hut. Now, I didn't hang out in the front; I stayed inside to avoid being spotted and punished by Mr. Terry. One morning, I came in the house at three or four again, and that did it. I overheard Mama make the phone call a few days later.

"Vickie, come get him before I kill him," she said. That's when I knew I was going to live with my mother and brother. I wasn't mad, but when Vickie came to get me, she was angry and fussing. I had to listen to her fuss all the way to Savannah.

In Savannah that fall, I hit the fifth grade recess rap scene. I soon found out that what had me on top in Waynesboro wasn't going to cut it in Savannah, so I had to change my game. I memorized a Fat Boys song and "Rapper's Delight" by The Sugarhill Gang, and dubbed myself M.C. Maurice. It wasn't long before I was gaining popularity because of my rapping skills, but I

36

failed fifth grade because of the turmoil I was dealing with at home. I loved Vickie and my baby brother, and I had looked forward to living with them, but she and I were fighting and arguing all the time.

The problems usually started because I retaliated against Jon for something he did to me, and Vickie always came to his defense. I understood that he was a little boy, but he shouldn't have been able to get away with everything. During one of the many arguments that happened when she tried to punish me unfairly, I yelled, "You treat Jon better than me because you like his dad!" I didn't expect the response I got.

"Your daddy raped me!" she screamed. Then she broke down in tears. I had no idea what that meant, but it had to be something bad. Whatever this man who was still a stranger to me had done to Vickie was the reason I got treated this way. It made me feel like I was something bad and there was nothing I could do about it.

At that time, Vickie had a boyfriend that I didn't like and who didn't like me, and that only made things worse. I didn't have a voice, and she seemed to believe what everyone else said instead of what I said. She was irrational, and I couldn't figure out how to be heard. After an explosive argument one night, Vickie put me out of the apartment, and I spent the night on the streets for the first time. At first, I begged to come back in, but she ignored me. Eventually, I started walking. I walked the streets for hours with nowhere to go. This wasn't right. I was ten years old, and there was no way Vickie could expect me to fend for myself. It was dark, and I had no money and no other family close by. Hours later, I returned to the apartment, but still wasn't allowed to come in. I curled up on the concrete stoop, leaned my head against the door, and slept until the sun came up.

When I heard movement inside the apartment, I started knocking again, begging to be let in so I could eat. At first, Vickie ignored me, but I kept knocking. When she finally opened the door, it was to throw a plate of eggs and bacon outside for me to eat like a dog. There was no spoon or fork, and I was starving by then, so I ate it with my hands. Eventually, she allowed me to come into the house and get ready for church. I had never felt so unloved before, and I was sure that Vickie hated me, but I didn't know why. I only knew that I couldn't live like this. That day in church, I prayed to God, asking him to let me live with Mama again. Eventually, I made it back to her, but the turmoil was far from over.

Chapter 5
I Do. Until I Don't.

Vickie

The most significant thing about my sophomore year at Georgia Southern College was that I met my first husband. I 'd had a few insignificant boyfriends by then, but didn't have a boyfriend at the time, and my male and female friends and I hung out in a group. Eventually, I dated a friend from that group named Antonio for six or seven months. He was in the army, and I was introduced to him by his sergeant. When Antonio left the army, we didn't try to maintain the relationship. Once Antonio was gone, my friendship with Desmond, a young man who had come to campus to build a repel tower for ROTC, grew. Desmond lived on base in Hinesville, Georgia, a small town about an hour and a half from GSC in Statesboro. We were still hanging out with a group of friends, but during a conversation alone one day, he let me know that he wanted someone he could settle down with, and build a family.

At some point during the discussion, I asked, "Well, do you have any prospects?"

"Yeah, you're the prospect," he told me. This was news to me. Desmond was a very handsome man, and I did like him, but he had a girlfriend who was also a single mother, and I respected that. He knew I had a son, of course, and had met Maurice when he visited me.

"Well," I told him, "you have a girlfriend, and as long as that's true, we can't be anything more than friends." As flattered as I was, I wasn't willing to be involved in a situation like that.

Eventually, Desmond and his girlfriend broke up, and he and I started dating in May of 1981. Our connection was strong, and we got married at the courthouse in Hinesville in August of that same year. I was 19 years old. He was serious about settling down and having a family, and I loved him enough to commit to being his wife. Once we were married, I moved into his home in

Hinesville. Desmond understood how important school was to me, so I commuted to GSC each day. I didn't tell my mother that I had gotten married. I knew she would disapprove - not because she was against me being married, but because she didn't want anything to take my focus off of my education.

Eventually, I admitted to myself that GSC wasn't where I was going to find my success. It's a great school, but there was just too much going on! I needed a smaller environment where I could have fun and still be academically successful. I also needed to attend school close to my new home because neither Desmond nor I liked the fact that I had to commute so far to go to class. We decided it would be best for me to take a break from school to concentrate on being a wife, and then re-enroll at a college closer to our home. I got a job working the night shift at a convenience store so that I could earn a little money while I was out of school. During that time, I determined that I had to get serious about my education. No matter what else was happening in my life, I had to make sure I was successful in college because, married or not, working low-paying jobs was never going to be enough to contribute to or sustain a family. I knew I wanted to keep the comfortable life style Mama had given me, and I believed her when she told me that education was the way to do it. Moreover, I was determined to not be the undereducated "statistic" so many people expected me to be.

One day, out of the blue, Mama and Aunt Sammie Joe showed up at Desmond's military formation in Hinesville. I don't know how they found him. He brought them to our home and we talked. Mama had been calling my dorm at GSC, and after not being able to reach me for a few weeks, she and my aunt drove to Statesboro to find out what was going on. They found out enough there to lead them to Hinesville.

"Vickie, please tell me you are not down here living with this man, and you're not married," Mama said.

"No, Mama, we're married," I confessed.

"Okay, good." I saw the stress leave her body as she breathed a huge sigh of relief. "You've got to have a wedding. Don't tell anyone you all are married until then. Agreed?" A wedding meant nothing to me, but was important to my mama and aunt, so Desmond and I agreed to keep our marriage a secret from those who didn't already know, and allowed the two women who had been most important in my upbringing to plan a small wedding for us. So, when I was 20 years old, Desmond and I had our wedding at Haven-Munnerlyn United Methodist Church in Waynesboro for a town full of people whose opinions I cared nothing about. Their attitudes had not mattered when I was a child, and they surely didn't matter now.

After being out of school for about a year, I chose to enroll at my mother's alma mater, Savannah State College, in Savannah, Georgia. She earned a degree in Elementary Education from SSC in 1955, and I decided to continue the legacy. Another reason I chose SSC was because it was only about 30 minutes from Hinesville, and had housing for married students. Desmond, Jon, and I lived there, and Desmond made the short commute to Hinesville each day.

I was now about a two and a half hour drive away from Waynesboro, and Maurice was a little older. Instead of going home every weekend, Maurice was able to visit me in Savannah more often. Sometimes my mother's friends from the neighborhood who were coming to Savannah would bring him along, and sometimes he would ride the Greyhound bus. He even spent summers with me at SSC and got a taste of the Tiger life as he played and rode his bike all over campus. We even went crabbing in the marsh behind Camilla-Hubert Hall. I hear him speak fondly of these moments even to this day.

I was pregnant with my second child by the age of 21. I knew that Desmond wanted a family, I agreed that this was the right time. Besides, Maurice had been begging for a baby brother for a while. On one visit to Waynesboro, Desmond and I pulled into the driveway and found Maurice talking to a small pecan tree in the backyard. "Why are you talking to the tree, baby?" I asked.

"Everybody's got a little brother but me," he told me sadly, "so I'm just talking to the tree."

I gave birth to my second child, Jon, in September of 1983. Thank God it was a boy.

41

This was a happy time in my life. I was married to a man I loved and who loved me, and I had two sons that I treasured. Unfortunately, the good times wouldn't last. Prior to his first long deployment to Germany, Desmond and I cried together for hours the night before he left. Since I was in school, I could not go with him then. He was extremely upset about having to leave me and our son, and I was just as upset at the thought of life without him. Our entire relationship had been a never-ending honeymoon, so knowing that we would be apart for so long was heartbreaking. The only thing that calmed him down was that I agreed to come to Germany when I graduated. We got very little sleep that night, unable to dwell on anything except our impending separation; the entire situation wrecked my nerves. I hated to see this man I loved so much go overseas without me, but I didn't see where I had a choice. I had two children and I was committed to earning my bachelor's degree.

Once Desmond was gone, I was living like a single mother of two, and I was a full time college student. Although Maurice wasn't residing with me, I was still responsible for him. I was done with the party scene by then, and I was far beyond many of the students on campus who were unmarried with no children, still enjoying the financial support of their parents. I made friends and they sometimes visited me at my home, but I still felt isolated. Desmond and I wrote letters and talked on the phone as often as possible. Time and distance didn't lessen our love for one another, and we longed for the time we could spend together on his semi-annual visits.

I finished my bachelor's degree as a married woman with two children. My mother was in her mid-seventies by then and unable to travel, so Aunt Sammie Joe and her husband, Uncle Alexander, attended the commencement ceremony at Savannah State College where I was the first and only graduate to earn a degree in Child Development and Family Services. Desmond was beyond excited that I had finally reached this goal. He had made provisions for us to join him in Germany. After searching for a job for me in Germany for weeks, he had finally found one that he thought I would enjoy.

As the time approached for me to go to Germany, I began to have second thoughts. I didn't doubt my love for Desmond, nor his love for me and Jon, but I didn't want to go all the way to Germany. The truth is, I didn't want to move that far away from my mother. If I did, there would be the inevitable battle over Maurice to consider. There was no way Mama would let him go with me. When Maurice was a toddler, an argument between Mama and me led to her pulling a gun on me - a rifle. I will never forget it. I sat on my bed as we yelled back and forth at each other before she appeared at my door with the rifle pointed at me. Maurice was in the room, but I wasn't worried about him. She would end her own life before putting his in danger. Aunt Sammie Joe stood behind her, trying to talk Mama into letting me live. "Matt Lee, put the gun down," she begged. "You don't want to do this."

"Yes I do, Sam!" Mama told her. "I'ma kill her dead! I'm tired of this!"

In my anger and youthful foolishness, I egged her on. "Yes, she does," I told my aunt. I looked at my mother. "Go ahead, shoot! You bad, shoot!" I dared her. She was tired of me talking back and being disrespectful, and I was tired of being treated like a child instead of a young adult. "Do it!" I screamed. They say God takes care of babies and fools, and the saying was surely true that day. Luckily, Mama harkened unto my aunt's pleas and let me live.

I couldn't leave Maurice behind while I went all the way to Germany, and I couldn't take him from Mama. We didn't have any communication at all with Phillip or his family, so I didn't have that to consider, but the bond Maurice and my mother shared was very strong, and I loved each of them too much to break it. Besides, Mama was aging, and I didn't want to be far away if anything happened.

When I told her about the decision I was trying to make, she said, "Baby, go with your husband." She expected Maurice to stay with her, of course. For her, it was as simple as that, but I just couldn't do it.

During one of our conversations, I finally told Desmond that I had decided to stay in Georgia and go to graduate school. For some reason, that was easier than telling him I didn't want to leave my mama. Needless to say, he was not happy. He said he didn't want to be married if he couldn't be with his family. I was hurt, but I understood. When he returned to the U.S., Desmond stopped in Savannah on his way to Massachusetts and we talked. I was actually relieved when he mentioned divorce; the stress of the distance and living as a single parent has taken its toll. The other reason I didn't balk at the idea was because it was supposed to be temporary; we believed that we would someday remarry. When it was all said and done, Desmond and I were married for seven years, but he was away on military duty for five of those. The divorce wasn't because our feelings had changed; we still loved each other very deeply. It was simply because I wouldn't travel to Germany and a long-distance relationship just didn't meet his needs.

We filed for divorce, but did so with the intention of re-marrying once he returned to the United States for good. In fact, we took a family picture on the day we filed the papers. When he came back from his last tour in Germany, however, he was seeing someone else, whom he eventually married. Although we'd continued to talk on the phone when he had gone back to Germany, it just hadn't been the same. In hindsight, I know that I should have gone to Germany after graduation as I had promised. Desmond loved me and he was a great father to both of my sons. All of the relationships I've had since then pale in comparison. I never found another love like that, and I never found a better man. He may never have found a comparable relationship, either, since he is currently on his fourth marriage. I wish him the best.

After graduation from SSC, I remained in Savannah and started to build a life there. I got a job with the Department of Defense as a Family Childcare Outreach worker. Maurice continued to visit regularly, but his behavior problems had gotten worse over the years. My mother and I were constantly on the phone about his misconduct, and she was becoming increasingly incapable of dealing with it. While he was still in elementary school, Maurice began staying out until three or four in the morning, doing God knows what. The streets were gaining control over my child, and there was little I could do to stop it from a hundred miles away, so Maurice came to live with me a few months into his fifth grade year and stayed with me through the following summer.

I wish I could say it was wonderful finally having Maurice with me, but it wasn't. I had never dealt with such defiance and disrespect. He rarely followed my directions and seemed to want to treat me as though we were equals. If I thought he was spoiled before, I was totally unprepared for what life would be like trying to raise Maurice alone. For almost eleven years, he had lived without responsibilities and had learned to talk his way out of any situation and talk Mama into giving him anything he wanted. Now here I was trying to hold him accountable for his behavior and make him do basic things related to his own care. Neither of us was prepared to live together. On a visit to Waynesboro at the end of the summer, Maurice refused to return to Savannah with me. It was late, and I didn't have time for a long fight, so Jon and I left Waynesboro without him.

The straw that broke the camel's back was when Maurice walked out of his sixth grade classroom and left the school campus without permission. He was 11 years old. When my mother sent him back to school, he talked to the principal, was punished, and left campus again. This time he absolutely refused to go back. At that point, my mother knew that she couldn't handle him anymore. I packed up his little brother, and we drove to Waynesboro to get him again. He was going to live with us from now on.

The earliest memory I have of Maurice's extreme defiance is when I told him to iron his shirt for school one morning. He refused. I repeated my directions, but he would not do as he was told, period. He talked back to me as though we were equals, and that was unacceptable. I was the parent; he was the child. I was completely caught off guard by how quickly things escalated. I don't remember who hit first, but blows were exchanged between us. I could never imagine hitting my mother, and I had no frame of reference for how to handle a child that would do such a thing. Although my younger son was just under three years old, we had established a standard parent/child relationship where I was respected and my directions were followed. This was a completely foreign concept to Maurice, and physical confrontation became a norm for us. I hated it, but I didn't know how to stop it. Sadly, incidents like the one that happened that morning would continue to occur for years to come.

Chapter 6
Between the Lions

Maurice

I had to go to summer school after fifth grade for the first time. That school year with Vickie had been wrought with arguments and fights, and it had affected my academic performance. I didn't want to repeat fifth grade, so I did whatever I had to do in summer school to make sure I passed.

The school I attended had a lion on each side of the platform at the top of the steps leading to the front door. Since Vickie had to drop me off early so that she could go to work, I had a couple of hours to practice each morning, and that platform between the lions was my stage. I worked it! People driving or walking by would stare, and at that point, I knew that I would eventually perform for a large crowd. I imagined myself with back up dancers and thousands of people screaming for me just as I had seen them do for Elvis, Michael Jackson, and New Edition. It was my first (imaginary) summer concert series.

On a visit to Mama's house in Waynesboro later that summer, I decided I wasn't going back to Savannah with Vickie. I couldn't; it was just too difficult living there. The environment was dangerous, volatile and unjust. So when it was time to leave Waynesboro, I refused. I wrapped myself around a bedpost and wouldn't let go. I knew Vickie had to get on the road and didn't have time to argue, so she ended up getting my things from the car and leaving me there.

Back in Waynesboro, my development as a rapper continued. In the sixth grade, my friend Chris Grubbs and I wrote a rap about peanuts for a contest sponsored by The 4-H Club, and we won first place. I continued to have behavior problems, though. After a confrontation with my sixth grade teacher one day, I left school without permission and walked home. I tried to explain why I left to Mama, but I didn't have the right words at the time to describe how the teacher had been talking down to me, and making comments tinged with racism and laced with contempt. Mama heard me out, but still called the principal, Mr. Roberts, and made me go back to school. When I got to Mr. Roberts' office, he listened to me, he talked to me, then he paddled me. Angered by the injustice of it all, I left again, and this time, I refused to go back. Mr. Roberts called my mama and told her they couldn't do anything with me and that I couldn't come back to that school, so towards the end of that school year I had to go back to Savannah to live with Vickie. I wasn't looking forward to that.

Within a few days, Vickie picked me up from Waynesboro. Of course, she was angry. When we arrived in Savannah, I saw that we would be living in a new apartment. That made me hopeful; I thought a new apartment meant a new start. I could not have been more wrong. It wasn't long before I knew then that nothing had changed and that I was going to be dealing with the same situation I had escaped the previous summer.

After one night in the new apartment, I was taken to the Charter Savannah Behavioral Health System treatment center. I had seen commercials that advertised this as a facility for adult mental patients, so I didn't know why we were there. It soon became clear that Vickie wanted me to stay there. I told her I didn't want to stay, so she took me back to the apartment. The next day, however, we were back at Charter and I was admitted. Jon was with us, and we all cried. I didn't want to be left there, and my brother didn't want to leave me. Vickie said she didn't want to leave me there, but she didn't know what else to do. Despite my pleas, she and Jon left, and I was placed in the care of strangers.

Hearing the doors close behind me as they took me deeper into the facility gave me a feeling of entrapment that I had never experienced before. I was overwhelmed by my emotions, and I cried for three days. I felt abandoned and thrown away. I knew Vickie wasn't right, but had no way to communicate it and no one to tell. I had no voice. Why was I there? Yes, I misbehaved and often didn't do as I was told, but I didn't think I had done anything to deserve that level of punishment. I didn't know anyone there, I was scared, and I wanted to get out.

I was exposed to a new level of dysfunction at the Charter treatment center, especially during group therapy sessions. Before going there, the only drug I knew about was crack, and I had no idea what it meant to molest someone. Now, among other things, I knew about heroin and cocaine, and that people violated children sexually. I couldn't grasp it all the first day; my head was swimming with all of this information, and my small town existence had not given me a frame of reference with which to understand it.

I met a boy named Andy who always had outbursts. He would scream and fight the adults. I saw orderlies and nurses strap Andy to a bed and give him shots to calm him down. I had never seen anything like that, and had never been in a place I couldn't leave. I felt alone, neglected, and confused by my presence there and everything I was seeing. Seeing Andy strapped down and injected let me know that I had to learn the game to get out of there. Bucking the system wasn't going to work anymore. I knew there were checkpoints and criteria that I needed to meet in order to be released, so instead of ignoring the rules as I normally would have, I played it cool. I attended group and one-on-one sessions with counselors and did whatever else I was told, but I wasn't perfect. I got in trouble the first week I was there for mooning the girls across the hall. I did it because my roommate did it, but the girls only told on me. That infraction caused me to lose my first family visit. Vickie was furious, but I was too hurt and angry to care.

"It's your fault I'm in here!" I told her during a phone call. "Come get me." My pleading fell on deaf ears. I remained at Charter for an entire month.

While there, I took classes so that I could pass the sixth grade. I was a smart kid, and I wanted to be in my right grade when I got out of there. The food at Charter was great, the craft/project classes were interesting, and I was still able to write raps and draw, but I didn't want to be there. I missed my mama, who I never got to talk to, and my brother Jon. Through the counseling sessions, and due to the nature of the program, I learned patience because, for the first time, I couldn't have what I wanted.

Mama wasn't there to give it to me or talk Vickie into giving it to me. Before that, I had learned to be persuasive and focused to get what I wanted; I never took no for an answer. Now, I didn't have a choice. Still, I was a child, and old habits are hard to break. For example, one of the rules was that we couldn't have food in our rooms, but my roommate and I devised a plan to keep Jell-O pudding cups in our nightstand drawers. I still broke a few rules, but was much smarter about it. That didn't stop me from getting caught, though, and I got in trouble again.

Vickie and Jon came to visit me, but the only thing I really remember about those visits is that they left without me. By the time I was released from the treatment center, I had learned skills that would help me circumvent confrontation. These skills were supposed to help me keep the peace between Vickie and me so that the fighting would stop. I was happy to be out of Charter and wanted to avoid another stay, so when Vickie yelled at me or was aggressive, I used my strategies. I counted to ten, wrote down my feelings, or beat up a pillow. Somehow, not engaging her seemed to have the opposite effect. She became more irrational, and my coping skills started to seem useless. Even her boyfriend, the same one who had mistreated me before, could see how she behaved towards me and became my advocate.

Nevertheless, I continued to draw and I still loved rap music. After leaving Charter, I stole magazines and drew pencil and pen graphics on poster boards Vickie bought for me, and hung them on my bedroom wall. When I started seventh grade at DeRenne Middle School in Savannah, I knew I had to do something special to make friends, so I decided to rap against the best kid in school. Most of the children I had known in sixth grade went to a different junior high school, so when there was a cipher on the playground, I jumped in. During a cipher, each person has to do a freestyle rap when it's their turn. I didn't win, but I wasn't mad. It just let me know that I had to step up my game.

Around the time, I heard that Sir Mix-a-Lot was earning $20,000 per show. That made me more determined to be a rapper. I needed to be able to take care of myself because I knew I couldn't survive living with Vickie forever. I met a boy named Calvin, and we decided to be a rap duo. All junior high school boys know that nicknames usually don't reflect your best attributes, so when I nicknamed Calvin "Cow-vin" because he looked like a cow, he wasn't mad, and when he nicknamed me "Moo-rice," I accepted the moniker in stride. On the bus from school that day, we tried many different names, but settled on Cow and Moo. It was much better than the stage name I had come up with when my friend, William, and I were planning to take over the rap world as M.C. Supernova and D.J. Big Bang a couple of years earlier. I liked learning and had always been interested in astronomy, so I looked in the encyclopedia when it was time to come up with names, and that's what we decided on. We might as well have called ourselves M.C. SuperNerd and D.J. Goofball.

When I left Savannah later that year, I chose to keep the nickname "Moo" just in case "Cow" ever wanted to find me. I had no way of knowing that name would last my whole life, and that I would land on Billboard's top 10 as M.C. Moo.

The other significant thing that happened that year was that I met Mr. Lamar, the career education teacher. I had never had a black male teacher before, and I was impressed by Mr. Lamar's clean cut look and the cool way he talked to us about life. On the first day of school, Mr. Lamar reprimanded me for talking. Everyone was watching to see how the new kid would handle this, so I had to choose to be a chump or be a man. I didn't take Mr. Lamar's reprimand in stride. I couldn't. Too much was riding on this.

"You talking to me?" I asked with my eyebrows raised and with just enough attitude in my voice for everyone to understand that what I really meant was, "*I know* you're not talking to me."

The look on Mr. Lamar's face let me know that was a mistake. "What, boy?"

Uh oh, I thought. I had to get out of this fast, but I didn't know how to because everyone was watching. "You don't have to talk to me like that," I told him. Wrong move.

"What?! Boy, are you crazy?" He stared at me as though he already knew the answer to his question. I gave him as much attitude as I could muster in response. This wasn't going well at all. "Come outside," he said.

On the inside, I was as scared as I had been of Mr. Terry when he found me at The Hut, but on the outside, I had to play it cool. So I stood up and sauntered out the door. I tried to stay tough as I stood face to face with this well-dressed, educated black man, but away from the gaze of my new peer group, I changed my tune, and Mr. Lamar gave me another chance instead of sending me to the office. Still, I earned a little schoolyard "cred" for not backing down - as far as they knew.

On the second day of school, I had a problem in the same class. I was in severe pain from stomach cramps. I was doubled over, and I asked Mr. Lamar if I could go to the clinic, but he said no. The pain was so excruciating that eventually I couldn't remain in my seat at all, so I rolled out of my seat and lay in the fetal position on the floor. Of course, Mr. Lamar wasn't having that.

"Boy, get up off the floor! Are you crazy?!" he yelled. I guess he asked a question instead of making a statement as a courtesy, and I wondered if he was going to ask me this every day.

I tried to explain that my stomach was hurting, but it didn't help. Already, I had gained the reputation of being "that kid," so I was sent to the office. The principal was a distant cousin, which only made things worse. She wouldn't cut me any breaks because she didn't want to be accused of showing favoritism. The principal called Vickie, and of course, she was angry at me. She just couldn't understand why I got in trouble at school, and I couldn't understand why no one cared that my stomach hurt so badly.

I was sent back to class, and as the day went on, my stomach pain diminished. By the time I got home that afternoon, it had almost completely subsided. When Vickie got home from work, I was sent to my room and stayed there for hours. She finally came into my room as the sun was setting, and she came in fussing.

"Look, Maurice, you are not going to do what you used to do," she began.

Again, I tried to explain that I had been in pain, but she thought I was just making trouble. While I was trying to make her understand what happened, she punched me in the jaw. It caught me completely off guard. It was the first physical abuse I had suffered at her hand since the fifth grade, and I cried. The tears weren't because the lick hurt; they were because of the overwhelming feeling of powerless I had. No one was listening to me - again. I was getting punished unjustly - again. This time, I didn't hit her back because I understood that retaliating only made things worse. She was my mother, and although the Charter treatment center strategies weren't keeping me from being abused, I didn't want to make it worse or end up back there. The blow to my face was followed by a verbal tirade laden with curse words and threats, but I didn't fight back. After a few minutes, Vickie's boyfriend came in and dragged her out of my room, leaving me confused, frustrated, and alone.

Unbeknownst to Mr. Lamar, he became my unofficial father figure/mentor. When I was in his class, I had never met my father, and it would be years before that would happen. I have a vague memory of asking where my father was as a very small boy, and being told that I didn't have one. Mr. Lamar was the one man I knew I would see every day who would answer my questions and give me advice. He taught us how to dress, how to conduct ourselves in job interviews, and how to do other things to be successful. It was in Mr. Lamar's class that I started thinking about owning a business, and my entrepreneurial spirit began to take shape. I didn't hold a grudge against him for sending me to the office that day; he had no idea what I was dealing with at home.

We moved around quite a bit during those years, and I continued to rap as I moved from school to school. I became good at being the new kid. Maintaining a certain perception helped me become well known. To fit in, I knew I had to be cool, dress well, and keep rapping. If I wasn't the best rapper when I arrived at a new school, I was the best when I left. I was now eating, sleeping and breathing rap. Kid 'n Play, Kwamé, Salt-N-Peppa, LL Cool J, Kool Moe Dee, Public Enemy - they were all shaping my style as a rapper. I had the rhymes, but I needed the look to go along with them. Mama could afford to keep me in certain clothes and shoes as the styles changed, but Vickie couldn't. Even when Mama was willing to buy me what I wanted, Vickie wouldn't always allow it. I grew to resent her for that. It was a very perplexing feeling for me because I always loved Vickie, but I had so many other feelings that resulted from our rocky relationship which often left me confused.

I didn't get to spend the entire school year with Mr. Lamar because we moved to Warner Robins, Georgia, during seventh grade, and in eighth grade, I started trying to set my own trend. I also started to realize I might actually be good at rapping. I wanted a demo recorded, but didn't understand the business and didn't know how to get it, so I just kept working on improving my skills. At home, life was horrible. Vickie had a few different boyfriends, and she and I were fighting constantly. The police were called regularly, and going to the Youth Detention Center (YDC) was becoming a normal thing for me. It seemed as though I was being punished for no reason, so I decided to give Vickie a reason. Either way, I was going to be punished, so I might as well get something out of it. I decided to do my own thing instead of following her rules, and I stayed out late. The less I was at home, the more I learned about the streets, mostly from a neighbor from Chicago named Kaz. Vickie didn't like him, but by this time, I didn't care.

No matter how much Mama pleaded, and no matter how much I begged, Vickie wouldn't send me back to Waynesboro. She would rather see me in the system than with Mama. I couldn't understand why. One night, when there was no room for me at the YDC, an employee from the Department of Children and Family Services (DCFS) allowed me to sleep in his home and took me to the judge the next day. I had appeared before this judge before, and this time, he sent me to foster care in Perry, Georgia. The same formula worked. I was cool, I dressed well, and I rapped. I rapped so well, in fact, that I became a part of The Show Dogs, a popular group at school.

Being in the foster home was okay. There were three other foster children, and we weren't treated poorly, but we were treated differently. Basically, we were treated like foster children. We were taken care of, but the family's biological children got more privileges and got more of the things they wanted. My foster

54

family was kind enough to give me a small party for my 14th birthday. I was able to visit Vickie and Jon on that day, too.

What affected my life most about living in foster care was that it was my first observation of a man as the head of a Christian household. Mama was a Christian, of course, but by the time I was born, my grandfather had been dead for years, so I was raised with a single female as the head of household. I always went to church on Sundays when I lived with Mama, and even when I lived with Vickie. I had always looked forward to the lock-ins and other activities for children at Overcoming by Faith in Savannah. But with this foster family, I attended church at least four days a week and listened as attentively as I could to the toothless preacher. I wondered why he didn't have dentures, but I didn't dare wonder this aloud.

Eventually, I was sent back home to Vickie. Not much changed, and I was still focused on rapping. In school, I created a rap group with two friends , B-Rock and E-Love. We must have been pretty good, because we won a rap contest and were scheduled to perform on the radio! I was the most excited I had ever been in my life. I was finally going to be on the radio, and I just knew this would lead to bigger and better things. I told Vickie the good news, but she was unmoved. We had a family counseling session the same day, so she said I couldn't go to the radio station.

No way. There was no way I was going to miss my big break. I begged her to just take me to the radio station first and then go to counseling. She refused, and we quarreled. On the way to counseling, I continued to beg and argue, but it fell on deaf ears. I just couldn't miss this chance. This was my group, my friends were depending on me, and Vickie was standing in my way. I had to do something. When we stopped at a traffic light, I jumped from the car and headed to the radio station. I could hear her yelling for me to come back, but I ignored her. This was just too important!

I ran as fast as I could to the radio station, but it was too late. B-Rock and E-Love had performed without me. I was hurt beyond words. I had wanted so desperately to hear myself on the radio, and Vickie had stood in my way. Why would she do something like this? Did she really hate me that much? I was devastated and angry. By then, she had told me over and over that being a rapper was a pipe dream. I was doing everything I could to make my dream come true, and it seemed like she was determined to do everything she could to stop it. That night, I was locked out of the apartment and had to sleep outside, again. This only added fuel to my dream and confirmed that I had to make it as a rapper to survive. I couldn't get to my mama, and no one else was going to take care of me, especially not Vickie.

When Vickie locked me out of the apartment this time, I didn't go home for a week, but I wasn't on the streets. I stayed with my friend Rashaad, and his sister, mother, and stepfather. They lived in the same apartment complex. At some point, Rashaad's mother talked to my mama who wired her money to buy clothes for me. As far as I know, Rashaad's mother never talked to Vickie, and I don't know where Vickie thought I was for a week. Eventually, when Vickie saw me in the complex one day, she asked me to come home.

A few days later, I went to see Rashaad, but he wasn't home. His mother was home alone, and she invited me in to talk. *Talk? To an adult? About what?* I hesitated. "You might have left some stuff here," she said. That was enough to get me into the apartment. "It's in my room," she continued. "Come on in."

She was my friend's mother and I trusted her, so I followed her into the bedroom she shared with her husband. She showed me a pair of shorts, and I told her they weren't mine. "You're handsome," she told me, switching subjects abruptly.

"Thank you," I replied.

"You're very handsome," she said again. It felt silly to say thank you again, so I remained quiet. "Do you think I'm pretty?" she asked. Her skin was light brown, she had freckles, and she wore her hair in dreads. I never considered whether or not she was pretty; she was just Rashaad's mom. She walked past me and closed the door, not waiting on a response. "Do you mind if I hug you?" she continued. I still wasn't catching on.

"Okay." She had taken care of me for a week, so I didn't think this was unusual. The hug was awkward, at best.

"Relax, don't be tense," she said. By then, I knew something wasn't right, but I didn't know what to do. I was only 14 years old and very inexperienced. The streets had taught me how to get a girl's phone number and maybe a kiss, but no one had told me anything about this kind of situation. As I stood there in her bedroom, she lifted up her t-shirt and started to take off her bra. I didn't want to see her breasts, so I looked away. Mentally, I was still a kid who enjoyed rapping and playing Nintendo games with my friends more than anything else.

"You ain't gotta look away. Don't be shy." I couldn't look, and I couldn't move. "Don't you want to touch these?" she asked as she sat topless on the foot of the bed.

"No, ma'am," I said. I had been raised to be respectful to adults, and even a situation like this one didn't change that.

"Aw, come on. Just feel 'em." Rashaad's mom grabbed my right hand and put it on her left breast. I wanted to be gone, but I literally couldn't move. *How am I going to get out of here?* I thought as she put my left hand on her other breast. As I stood there with my arms outstretched, held in place by her grip, my mind raced to come up with a way to leave before things got worse. I didn't want to be disrespectful, but I couldn't stay. This wasn't right.

When I didn't respond, she stood up and kissed me. I clamped my lips shut so that she couldn't stick her tongue in my mouth. She let go of my wrists and grabbed me between my legs. My hands remained on her breasts in an effort to keep some space between us. Puberty doesn't care about right or wrong, so, although I was scared and disgusted, my body responded to her groping. Then she started trying to unzip my shorts. *I've got to get out of here!* I searched frantically for the right thing to say - something that wouldn't anger her and make her more aggressive, and wouldn't hurt her feelings or embarrass her. This was my friend's mother, after all.

She kept talking as she fumbled with my belt and zipper. "Do you know how long it's been since a man touched my breasts? Do you know how long it's been since my husband had sex with me?" she asked. I didn't know the answer to either of these questions, and I wasn't going to stay around to find out.

"My mama's looking for me," I told her. "I have to go now." This was the typical version of "my mama said" that children used when talking to adults whom they thought wouldn't listen otherwise.

"Aw, stay a while longer," she begged. There was a pleading in her eyes and voice that made me feel sorry for her, but not sorry enough to stay.

"She said I could only stay for five minutes," I lied. "I have to go or she's gonna be mad." When she didn't move, I added, "I'll come back."

"You promise? Do you promise to come back?" she asked. She had stopped trying to unzip my shorts, and I took a step back and re-buckled my belt. She stared at me, waiting on my response.

"Yes, ma'am, I'll come back." That false promise and the possibility that Vickie would come looking for me were the only reasons Rashaad's mom let me out of her room. She didn't follow me as I headed straight for the front door. Although I hadn't done anything wrong, I felt dirty and ashamed, like it was my fault for going in there. I was also worried about losing Rashaad as a friend and having to fight her husband if either of them ever found out. If Rashaad or his stepfather had a concern about me being in their apartment, it was probably related to Rashaad's sister. Neither of them ever guessed that it was the mother, not the daughter, that posed the problem.

When I got home, I washed my face and hands, and scrubbed my mouth. I didn't tell Vickie what happened. We already had problems, and she probably would have blamed me because everything seemed to always be my fault. We traveled to Waynesboro that same day, and the memories of that afternoon tormented me. I never went to Rashaad's apartment again, even when he invited me. I just made up an excuse of some kind. His mother acted as though nothing had happened, and never did more than speak to me after that horrible day.

Life went on. Every year, I set goals for myself related to rap. Doing well in school was a given and I excelled academically no matter what was going on at home. The only thing that negatively affected my academic performance was all of the moving around we did.

The next year, we moved from luxury apartments to lower end apartments. I supposed it was because Vickie couldn't afford the rent anymore and it cost less to live there. As always, she took her stress out on me. The string of bad relationships didn't help, either. When it came to her boyfriends, I didn't like them and they didn't like me. Vickie never defended me against their teasing and taunting, and when I defended myself, I was put out of the house, sometimes overnight.

Still, I rapped. I started a new group with two new friends. We called ourselves S.F.C., Strictly for Chillin' and even had t-shirts made with our names on the backs. My stage name had morphed into "The Moo," so that's what I had on the back of my shirt. Another altercation with Vickie led to me being sent back to my church-loving foster family for three months, and back to my previous middle school. At school, I played it cool and stayed positive. I never talked about my home life, so I always believed that no one knew what I was going through personally. That belief was shattered when I got into an argument with a girl at school one day. I don't remember everything about it, but I'll never forget that she said, "That's why you a foster child. Everybody know yo' mama don't want you." Her words stung. I tried to retaliate, but my comeback was weak. I had no idea that anyone knew anything about me outside of school, and finding out in such a public way left me embarrassed, ashamed, and hurt.

Shortly afterwards, I returned to Vickie's home. It wasn't long before I was sent to the Georgia Industrial Home for Boys in Macon, Georgia, after another explosive incident that landed me in court. S.F.C. dissolved because of my constant movement from one foster home to another. I was able to work at the home for boys to save money to buy school clothes, and of course, I rapped. I made sure I had my M.C. Hammer pants, which every serious rapper had to have, and I won every rap battle. I learned that I was a good rapper, a good writer, and a good artist. I was very creative and thought about things differently. I was not a follower, but it would be years before I learned to lead in a positive direction.

On one of my visits home, Vickie was dating a man named Ethan. I disliked him from the moment I met him. He was sheisty and I saw him for what he was immediately. Still, when she asked if I wanted to move to Beaufort, South Carolina, with them, I said yes. At the time, I still hoped that she and I could re-establish the relationship from my younger years, and I wanted to be around my little brother. Unfortunately, Vickie married Ethan when she found out she was pregnant, and now I had problems from both of them. Ethan was a bad influence, to say the least. He did bad things, taught me bad things, and blamed me for the bad things he did. If I was headed down the wrong path before he came, there was no way I was going to get on the right one with him present.

One of my friends and I had something we called the Wonder Dollar Trick. We put tape on the end of a dollar and inserted it into a change machine. When it triggered the machine to give us the change, we would snatch it back out and do it over again to get more money. I showed Ethan how to do it, and he was impressed. He did the Wonder Dollar Trick every chance he got. One day, Vickie found one of his wonder dollars and asked why the money had tape on it. Ethan said he had taken it from me when he caught my friend and me trying to rob a change machine. Luckily, she believed me when I told her the dollar wasn't mine. This wouldn't be the last time he blamed me for something he did.

Ethan and Vickie fought, and I hated him for it. No matter how she treated me, she was still my mother and I couldn't stand to see anyone hurt her. Even though she and I fought, it was only to defend myself and I never felt good about it. I loved her and knew it was wrong, but didn't know what else to do. Not fighting back didn't lessen the severity of the beatings. During one of our conflicts when I was about 11, I chose not to fight back. Instead, I ran into the bathroom, and she followed me. As I tried to escape the forceful blows of the belt, I fell into the bathtub. She kept swinging as I screamed and cried. I don't remember why Vickie was angry with me that day, but I remember that she beat me so viciously that I bled. My blood pooled around me in the tub as I cried and begged her to stop. I don't know why, but she eventually stopped striking me. Maybe she thought she had killed me.

Ethan found out early on that fighting with Vickie didn't mean an easy win, if he won at all. Still, I tried to defend her sometimes, and he and I tussled. I decided I had to get him out of our lives, so on a visit to Waynesboro, I got a gun off the streets. Ethan was a threat to our safety, and I had to do something about it. When I left Waynesboro and returned to Beaufort, it was my full intention to get him out of the house and out of our lives by any means necessary. Fortunately, Vickie found the gun before I could use it. If he hit her or me again, I would have killed him and she knew it.

Whenever I had been the new kid before, things had gone well. Beaufort, South Carolina, was the first time the other kids had a different response to M.C. Moo. The girls still liked me, but instead of the boys wanting to be down with me, they wanted to fight. One night, some friends and I walked a girl home. I wasn't supposed to leave the house because I was babysitting my little brother, but it wasn't dark yet and I planned to come right back. So I left Jon at home and went with my new friends. A short while into the walk, I was jumped by three older boys that I knew, and the "friends" I had been walking with didn't help me. I was hit, kicked, and burned with cigarettes. I fought back, but I lost; it was one against three, and I hadn't even seen the first punch coming. I hadn't been hurt this bad since I had been hit in the face with a bottle in sixth grade. I was playing in the projects and a boy tried to take the batteries out of my boombox. I fought him, and when his brothers jumped in, I fought them, too. As I was walking away with my boombox and batteries in hand, someone yelled out my name. The boy who tried to take my batteries had thrown a glass bottle, and when I turned around, it hit me on the left side of my face. I developed a huge pocket of bruised blood that I had to have drained a few days later. I still have the scar.

After I was jumped that night in Beaufort, one of the boys I had been walking with helped me home. I must have looked horrible because Jon panicked, and when Vickie came home and found me on the couch bruised, bleeding, and burned, she was horrified. She took me to the emergency room where I was treated, and we pressed charges. Uncle Don and Mama drove up to see about me. Because of her health and age, it was one of the rare times Mama came to visit us where we lived. A few weeks later, I went to court about the incident and the judge fined my attackers. They later apologized, but never offered a reason for the attack. Strangely, the bruises and cuts increased my popularity at school, and I ended up with a few much older friends.

Vickie had come to my rescue then, but she and I continued to fight, and I continued to fight Ethan, too. Sometimes, when I came to her defense against him, she defended him against me. Following one of these times, my friends came to my aid. This particular fight had spilled outdoors, and once the word got out that a grown man was fighting me, my friends used their cars to barricade the entrance to the apartment complex where we lived, and surrounded Ethan. It became clear that Ethan was going to go down, and that was too much for Vickie, so she called the police *on me.*

When the police arrived, there was a standoff. I didn't want my friends hurt or in trouble, so I told them to move their cars. Once the police got into the complex, Vickie told them I was crazy and that she wanted me evaluated. I can't describe the hurt and betrayal I felt that she would try to have me institutionalized again. Hadn't Charter been enough? It seemed as though it didn't matter who I was fighting against or why, she would never take my side, even when I fought for her. At Vickie's request, the police took me to the hospital instead of jail. At that point, I didn't know which was worse. As I rode in the back of the police car, I could see my friends following us all the way to the hospital. They wouldn't leave until I was let go. I had never experienced anything like that before; I had a large loyal following. I wasn't sure how I had gotten it, but I knew I liked it.

The doctors at the hospital determined that there was nothing wrong with me. Soon after that, I was finally sent back to Waynesboro to live with Mama. The day before I left, Vickie had to take me to the hospital again, this time for a broken wrist I got in a fight with a neighborhood kid. Vickie and Ethan had two children together, my sister and youngest brother, and divorced a few years later. He is still one of my least favorite people.

I was happy to be back with Mama, but my conduct didn't improve. You would think that I would be on my best behavior since I was out of the abusive environment, but it just wasn't that simple. I was in turmoil on the inside, and I didn't know who to talk to or what to say, so it manifested in negative ways. When a teacher wouldn't give me permission to go to the restroom, I left the classroom anyway and got suspended. It wasn't long before I ended up in the Youth Detention Center for stealing something out of a mailbox with a friend while I was suspended from school. Mama couldn't stop the misbehavior, and although she didn't want to, she sent me back to Vickie who now lived in Sumter, South Carolina.

The moves from Beaufort to Waynesboro to Sumter, along with all of the problems I was experiencing, caused me to have to repeat ninth grade. I was devastated and embarrassed. I thought that having to repeat a grade made me look dumb, and being dumb wasn't cool.

In Sumter, I started rapping with another friend. When there was a talent show at the junior high school, we asked to be in it. Once we had permission, we went all out. We even had backup dancers for the first time, and we won the talent show! The feeling I had was better than playing the tambourine in my gray suit and Michael Jackson church glove in the school play. Winning that talent show helped me make up my mind to go hard for my dream.

Another major thing that happened during my time in Sumter was that my brother Jon's dad, Desmond, came to visit. When he arrived at the house, he picked up Jon and left me. I knew that Desmond wasn't my father, but he was the closest thing to it I had ever known, so it hurt when I was left behind. I had never met my father, and it was clear that Ethan wasn't going to be a father to anyone, not even his own children. When Jon went to spend time with Desmond, I knew no one was ever going to do that for me. I didn't tell Vickie how I felt about being left behind until years later.

During one of the rare good times in our relationship, Vickie took me and a friend of mine to a concert featuring B Angie B, Special Generation, and Joey B. Ellis. I had a great time, but seeing others on stage doing what I wanted to do wasn't enough for me. After the show, I talked my way backstage and met with Peter Seven of Bust It Records, M.C. Hammer's label. He gave me his business card and told me to send him a demo. That card was better than one of Willie Wonka's golden tickets. I had a record executive's business card - my dream was within my reach!

Within days, I recorded "Step to This" over Paris' song, "The Devil Made Me Do It." Since I didn't have any real equipment, I used two tape recorders - one to play Paris' song while I rapped, and the other to record it all. I did it without making a single mistake. When I was finished, I wrapped the cassette in a brown paper bag, addressed it, kissed it, and prayed for a record deal. I never heard anything from Peter Seven.

I spent my second year of ninth grade back in Waynesboro at Burke County High School. Mama had purchased a program called "Where There's a Will, There's an A" to help me catch up in school. I was on it! At this point, education was still important to me, and I didn't want to look stupid, nor did I want to fail again. I wanted to be a rapper, but not a dumb rapper. Sometime during the school year, I received a rejection letter from Bust It Records. I was disappointed, but strangely enough, it motivated me. I had a real letter from a real record label! Instead of discouraging me, it made me want to go harder. At the same time I was reading "Word Up!" magazine and seeing people from Augusta on its pages, like label owner Tony Mercedes and the group Simply Smooth. All of this fueled my dream.

The Wild Man Ron Thomas was the deejay on the local radio station that played rap music. I called in to the show so much that he made me the official school news person. Whenever he was doing a remote broadcast, I followed him around to get free stuff and he got to know me. Once he saw my popularity, he gave me a job as a deejay on Saturdays. I probably earned minimum wage, but I didn't care; I loved the music and notoriety so much that I would have done it for free.

When Simply Smooth came to Waynesboro to perform, I challenged a New Jersey rapper named Lord who performed in that show. I took a chance because I didn't know if I was better than him or not, but it paid off. Lord, whose real name is Troy Gattis, eventually produced my song, "I'm the Moo-nificent." When I asked my mama for money to go into the studio to record it, she said, "Go hand me my pocketbook." No questions asked. She always believed in my dream, and whenever I asked her for help achieving it, her response was the same.

Once the song was recorded, I listened to it repeatedly in Uncle Don's truck. I sat in that cab and let it play over and over again. Hearing it filled me with a great sense of accomplishment. I had no money and no record deal, but I wasn't memorizing other artists' raps anymore as I had done in elementary school, and I didn't have to keep participating in schoolyard ciphers to prove myself. I had my own demo! This was a first among my friends and was a major feat for a second-time ninth grader.

I gave the demo to Wild Ron and he promised to play it on his radio show that night. I listened for what seemed like forever, and then I heard it. My song was on the radio and I was thrilled! A few years before, Vickie had cost me my chance to be heard on the radio with my friends, but this was so much better. Within seconds, my phone was ringing off the hook. I answered a few calls, but when my song ended, I stopped answering the phone and went outside. I walked down the street and got my props from everyone in the neighborhood. I was loving it!

I passed the ninth grade that year and kept on writing rap songs. That summer, a show featuring Prince Raheem, M.C. Nas-D and DJ Freaky Fred, and Kilo came to our high school for a concert, and I was their opening act. This was it! My dream was becoming a reality, and I wanted to do everything I could to reach the top. I decided I needed backup dancers again, so I got five friends from the neighborhood and we practiced for hours on end.

That show changed my life. When I hit the stage, the response from the crowd made it official: I was a rapper. All other creative outlets took a backseat to writing and performing rap songs. From that point on, I went at it every way I could. Mama continued to support me, and I felt like I was proving Vickie wrong with every small success. This was not a pipe dream, this was real! As all of these wonderful things were happening for me, I shared them with Vickie, but I didn't get much of a reaction. She still couldn't see it.

During Christmas break that year, I had the opportunity to fly to New York to record a song. I went to my mama. "Go get my pocketbook," she said. No questions. I flew to New York and recorded with Lord and some of the local talent. When I arrived, I had a rap prepared, but as I listened to other rappers, I decided not to use it. Their material was better, so I had to come up with something on the spot. When it was my turn, I stepped into the booth and killed it! That's when I learned to step my game up based on my environment. Years of playground rap battles had prepared me for on-the-spot challenges, and I came correct. I was sixteen years old and living my dream!

My experience in New York was one I will never forget. While I was there, I wanted to see the ball drop in Times Square on New Year's Eve. I had seen it many times before on TV and was determined to see it live. On the way to Times Square, we stopped at Lord's friend's house. Lord's friend was a DJ and had crates of music lining almost every wall from floor to ceiling, and he had turntables. I had never seen anything like it and was immediately enthralled. Needless to say, I didn't go to sleep that night, but I never saw the ball drop, and I didn't care. I was energized by my love of music and instead of leaving New York with the memory of the ball dropping in Times Square etched firmly in my memory, I left with a ton of mix tapes.

Even though my rap career was taking off, I was still concerned about school and wanted to graduate. With everything I had going on, I figured I'd need a tutor to finish, but I never thought about dropping out.

Because of Mama's health, we didn't have a car. Uncle Don had traded in the one we had for a truck, so when we needed food, I had to walk to the grocery store and carry everything back. Most other errands were handled the same way. Sometimes my great Aunt Sammie Joe would take me on errands for us, and my uncle helped sometimes, too, but he lived 30 miles away. I had been asking for a car for a while and finally got one at 16 years old. After she spoke to Mr. Patterson, a neighbor who worked at the local car lot, Mama sent me to get it. At her request, Mr. Patterson, who was also my childhood friend William's grandfather, chose a "good car" for us - a 1986 4-door Buick Century.

That car changed the game. Almost immediately, I lost focus on school and became more focused on music and girls. I was supposed to keep riding the bus to school and only drive the car for errands, but I went against Mama's rules and drove the car to school instead. On Saturdays, I would drive around with my friends or hang out at the mall to meet girls instead of going to my job at the radio station. When I noticed all of the attention rappers and singers were getting from girls because of the backstage passes they wore, I had some made. My new group, M.C. Moo and the Innocent Criminals, with Farmer Brown as our hype man, was featured prominently on the fake passes. Eventually, I started skipping school and driving to schools in other counties to meet girls. One morning I woke up and decided I was bored with school, but kind of kept going. Needless to say, I failed tenth grade, but this time it didn't bother me as much. I was a popular (but still unpaid) rapper, and doing well in school didn't fit that image.

By now, I was performing at all of the local shows in Waynesboro, Augusta, and surrounding areas. When I saw the rapper Too Short perform, I was entranced by the gold and diamonds he wore. I think the bling made me ignore the change that was happening in rap music. The popular sound had changed from hip-hop to bass music, but I hadn't changed with it. My first time on stage at Club Mercedes, where most performers did shows, I got booed. I knew I could rap, so I ignored the response because I didn't understand commercialized music versus good rapping. Around the same time, The owner of the club, Tony Mercedes, put together a group called Duice. When I heard their demo for a song called "Dazzey Duks," I didn't think much of it and was surprised when it became a big hit a couple of months later. I was a rapper; I used metaphors and similes and drew relationships between seemingly unrelated things. What I was hearing had no substance, but it was selling.

Watching more and more artists become successful performing these kinds of songs was the turning point of my style. I switched from quality hip-hop to bass music. One of my earliest attempts was a song I wrote titled "One Leg Up." I went to my mama again. "Hand me my pocketbook," she said. Uncle Don took me to his friend Tony Scott's studio where I recorded the song, but I didn't copyright it. My song was stolen and, admittedly, improved. It became a big hit. I learned that I was still too lyrical for bass music. I also learned that the music business was a dirty game. This would not be the last time I learned this lesson.

Still, I chased my dream. I was a good rapper, but I wanted to be better. When I started my second year of tenth grade, I decided that I needed a radio and CD player in my car. I had been fired from the radio station for missing too many days, so I didn't have my own money, but I was used to getting what I wanted and didn't see why that should change now. I asked my mama for it, but she said no, so on the way from my girlfriend's house one night, I stole a Slim Jim from a store. Then I went to the same lot where my car had been purchased, broke into a car, and stole a radio. I knew exactly what I wanted. What I didn't know was that the police were staking out the car lot, and I was apprehended immediately. The owner of the car lot pressed charges, and my tenure on the wrong side of the law began. At the age of 17, I was charged and placed on first-offender probation. It was possible to have my record expunged if I didn't commit another crime while on probation.

School was secondary by this point, and it wasn't long before I got put out for good. It started one morning when a white boy called a friend of mine a nigger. The institutional racism I experienced in school and in Waynesboro in general was overwhelming, and the verbal disrespect that day was the straw that broke the camel's back. After months of attending a school where black boys were always being accused of doing things we hadn't done, being searched without cause, and being treated like second class citizens who didn't belong in the newly-built county high school, we decided to fight back by beating up everybody white. It seems foolish now, but as an angry teenager at an integrated school with white administrators in a small, barely integrated town, we didn't know what else to do, and we obviously didn't consider the consequences. We started with whoever was standing near us and fought our way to the front office. That's where the real problem was. Some of the white students were okay, but the administrators were barely able to hide their disdain for us, and we were tired of being treated like that. So when I said, "Hey, y'all, Let's go get Mr. Arnold!" no one hesitated.

About 15 of us swarmed the office. "What are you doing in here?" the secretary asked. The question was barely out of her mouth before somebody punched her in it. Three of us ran past her and jumped Mr. Arnold, the racist principal. He was the worst of them all, so he got the worst beating. Everyone else who happened to be in the front office caught the brunt of our anger, too. We weren't trying to kill anyone, but we wanted them to feel physical pain akin to the mental and emotional angst we had been feeling for years.

After we had done all the damage we could do, we headed for the door, but it was locked. That stopped us in our tracks. "Open the door!" we screamed at the crying secretary. She was crouched on the floor, afraid to move.

"I can't," she sobbed. "They've locked us in from the outside!" Uh-oh. We hadn't anticipated this.

"Let us out!" we yelled as we shook the doors, trying our best to escape the scene of our attack.

"We are not opening the door until the police get here," someone responded from the other side. The police had been called, and campus security kept us locked in the front office until backup arrived. Amazingly, I was taken home instead of being taken to jail. I didn't recognize who I had become, but I realized I had finally found a crew to run with. We were all put out of school for attempting to incite a riot. I didn't care about anything that had happened at school or the consequences, but Mama's disappointment hurt me deeply.

69

Slowly, I was starting to live the street life and was becoming more aware of the seriousness of it. A good guy from our community was shot and killed when I was 16. His senseless death had been the result of an argument. "Kill or be killed" was becoming the mantra of every wannabe thug, and my life was headed in the same direction.

Mama tried to take me back to school after about a week, which meant either she would advocate for me no matter what, or that she had grossly underestimated my role in the attack on the principal. The answer from administration was a solid "no." The principal said I was a menace to the Burke County school system and couldn't come back. Ever. That meant I had to go to school in a neighboring county if I wanted to continue my education, which is what Mama wanted. I didn't transfer to another county immediately, though. I chilled for a while, writing raps and doing what I wanted to do. I admit that I was belligerent and disobedient, but I thought I was a man, and men did what they wanted to do, not what their grannies told them to do.

By this time, we had home healthcare for Mama. The home health worker that was coming to the house was very caring toward my mama, and very nice to me. It came as a total shock when I discovered she was my aunt. I don't know why she chose not to tell me during all of those visits to our house, but she never did until after Vickie told me that the woman coming to our house every day was my father's sister. A short while after that, Vickie called me and said, "I think it's time for you to meet the other side of your family. Do you want to meet your other grandmother?"

I said yes. "Okay," she replied. "I'm coming home, and I'm taking you to meet your father's people." And just like that, I was going to have the other pieces of my puzzle. I was excited, and I had countless questions.

As promised, Vickie came home for a visit and took me to Pabunkee, Georgia, about 20 miles from Waynesboro, to meet my father's family. I was nervous. We didn't talk much on the way, so I had no idea how she was feeling. When we pulled into the dirt driveway, an old woman came out of the house and met us in the yard. "That's your grandmother," Vickie said as she approached. I

70

looked at the house and the woman, and realized I'd been there before. When I was three or four years old, Vickie had brought me there after an argument with Mama, and when she said she was leaving me with this strange woman, I screamed and cried, and wasn't forced to stay. The long-forgotten memory came back to me as I stared at the old house whose screened front porch was furnished like the inside of a home.

Rosie Knight, my paternal grandmother, walked up to me as I got out of the car. "Let me see your hands," she told me. I held them out and she looked at my palms. "Yep, you mine," she said. I had no idea what that meant. Years later, I found out that my father's mother had dark palms, and the trait showed up in her offspring. My dark palms were enough proof for her that I was a part of her family.

Within the next couple of months, I met other aunts, uncles, and cousins, but not my father. Meeting my father's family was weird. I knew we were all related, but we had no emotional bond. Standing in a room full of them was surreal. On one visit, a kid approached me cautiously. He was short, dark-skinned and chubby, and his smile was infectious. "You my brother?" he asked. I'm sure he had been told that before I arrived, but kids like to verify things.

"Yeah," I told him, and gave him a hug. He was happy to have a big brother, and I was used to being that for Vickie's three other children, so I embraced that role. All of the cousins I met that day were younger than me. There was only one older than me, but I didn't meet him until I was a much older adult because he lived out of state. I made subsequent trips to Pabunkee on my own because Vickie refused to be around my father's sisters. They had never apologized for the brutalization in high school, and she wasn't up for pretending everything was all good.

I started spending time at my new Aunt Mary's house in Augusta. She had three boys, and hanging out with my younger cousins was fun. Since my Buick wasn't working, Aunt Mary let me use her car to take a friend named Demetria to a military ball, but I had to pick up the car at my new Aunt Natalie's house. When I called Aunt Natalie to tell her I would be picking up the car and to arrange a time, she told me that my father would be there. I would finally meet him. Any nervousness I felt about the military ball was replaced by anxiety about meeting my father. This was different than meeting my other relatives. I didn't know what to do or say when I saw him, so I decided to just let it happen.

Later that evening, I was at Aunt Natalie's house getting dressed in my tuxedo and heard his voice. I didn't know what to do. Should I wait for him to come in, or should I go outside? No one came in, so once I was dressed, I decided to go outside. I tried to anticipate the conversation, but that was impossible. I had nothing to base it on, so I had no idea what to expect. Aunt Natalie introduced us.

"Maurice, this is your dad." Just like that, after 16 fatherless years, the missing puzzle piece was put in place. We stared at each other in the front yard. *I don't look anything like him*, I thought.

Finally, he spoke, greeting me very formally. "Hello, how are you doing?" I told him I was fine, and the next few minutes were filled with insignificant small talk. He seemed to be unsure if I was his son. I didn't ask any questions, and headed to the military ball soon after. He gave me some money before I left. I pushed any feelings I had aside and enjoyed myself at the ball.

My next interaction with my father was on Thanksgiving Day at Aunt Natalie's house where everyone gathered. My paternal grandmother and all of my aunts were incredible cooks, and I loved sharing meals with them. When my father arrived, an older relative whom I'd just met that day asked, "So this is your oldest son?"

"That's what they say," my father said. "I don't know." I took that as my cue to leave.

"I don't have to take this," I said as I got up from my chair. "You ain't never done nothing for me."

"No, Maurice, please sit down," my grandmother said. "You're here for me." Initially, I refused, but I decided to stay when she kept asking. She had never been anything but kind to me, and I couldn't tell her no.   Over the next few years, my grandmother and I developed a relationship that I value greatly. I

72

had some reservations at first, because I didn't want the one who raised me to feel like I had betrayed her somehow, but she never had a problem with it. She knew my love for her would never change.

A few months later, a conflict over my girlfriend led to me shooting at a friend of mine with a borrowed gun. This girl was my first "serious relationship," and when I found out she was messing around with my friend, I felt betrayed. This is what made me finally decide to drop out of school. She attended the school I had been expelled from, and going to school in another county made it impossible to watch her and keep her from cheating again. But I wasn't a killer. I wanted to hurt my friend for his betrayal, but I didn't want to see him dead. When the confrontation finally happened, my aim wasn't steady and I didn't mind that I missed him. Yet, he retaliated. He and a friend were waiting outside my house one night when I came home. They ran when I saw them.

I called the police and said, "Look, Christopher Smith was waiting outside my house when I came home and I'm about to go kill him."

The officer's response was, "Well, if you're gonna kill him, what are you calling us for?" I took that as permission to handle my business, and this time, I wouldn't miss. On my way to Christopher's house, I saw that the police had him pulled over. They probably saved both of our lives that night.

God knows I wish I had listened to my mama, but the pulse of the streets was too strong. Dr. Dre and Snoop were my mentors at that time. Even though drugs had never been my thing, I went to school wearing a "Legalize Today" t-shirt. I was quick to fight and wasn't scared to shoot, but I never did drugs and didn't drink alcohol. The most important thing was for me to keep my "street cred" up and my rap game hot. I felt like my hard work was finally starting to pay off when Carlton Allen of LaShawn Records gave me my first record deal after I won a talent show at Imperial Theatre in Augusta. A record deal! No money exchanged hands, but I was a signed artist nonetheless.

This was a happy time in my life. I was so focused on my music career and new girlfriend that I hadn't been going to see my probation officer. When I stopped at a local restaurant to eat one night, I was surrounded by police because I hadn't been checking in. When they searched my car, they found a gun I had bought off the streets and I was charged with possession of a firearm by a first offender. That gun was the second one I had owned since the one I bought to defend Vickie and me against Ethan, but I always had access to guns. Everyone did.

Carlton Allen wrote a letter to the judge and I was released on intensive probation as I awaited my court date. I had to be in the house by 7 pm each night, which is almost impossible for a teenager who had been living my life up until that point. Needless to say, I had a host of violations during this time. Once, I even ran into my probation officer at a night club.

Nonetheless, I didn't want to go to jail. I could never stand to be caged. As a toddler, I remember being left alone in my crib, which was placed against a wall in my bedroom. Mama and Vickie were trying to teach me to sleep by myself. I cried and screamed, and when no one came, I kicked the slats out of the side of the crib and broke free. The next night, Vickie turned the crib around so that the broken slats faced the wall. I kicked the other side out, too. Like I said, I couldn't stand to be caged. To me, jail was no different. If I violated the law, it wasn't because I didn't care about being locked up; I just thought I could beat the system. I had lived my life on second chances and being able to talk my way out of things, and I expected that strategy to keep working. To improve my chances of avoiding real jail time, I took the GED test before going to court, and I talked to a recruiter from DeVry University about attending college in Atlanta. I always knew education was important, and even though I had dropped out of school, I could see that my current plan wasn't working. I was still performing in local shows while I waited to go to court.

When the court date arrived, everyone was there: Mama, Vickie, and Uncle Don. The last time I'd stood before this judge, my lawyer had told him that I wouldn't be back, yet here I was. Although I had violated probation, I had also taken the GED exam and was planning for college. I felt like I had a chance. When it was time to hear from my family, Vickie spoke, and I could almost see any chance I thought I had dissipate.

"Maurice is hardheaded and doesn't listen," she told the judge. "He violates probation by leaving the house after check in." *What?* I couldn't believe this! It seemed like she was doing everything she could to get me locked up. Anger and resentment rose in me like a flood, but I remained quiet as she continued her plot against me. "My mother is too old to handle him, and I want to take him back with me," she said before taking her seat. *No way!* I thought. I knew that wouldn't work because our relationship hadn't improved and she was still married to Ethan. I was older, taller, and stronger than I had been when I left Sumter, and there was no way the three of us would survive living together.

The next person to speak was the senior probation officer. She recommended that I get locked up. Period. She was sure I would continue to offend if I wasn't.

When it was my turn to speak, I said, "I don't wanna go with my mother; we don't get along. I passed my GED test and I plan to go to college." I went in to a little more detail about how I had changed, how I wanted to do better, and the steps I had already taken, but the judge was not convinced. I'd stood before him one too many times. He sentenced me to 360 days in the Emanuel Probation Detention Center in Twin City, Georgia, miles away from my sick and aging mama who had remained silent during the proceedings.

When the judge handed down the sentence, Vickie had the nerve to cry. They were probably tears of joy. "It's your fault," I told her as I was taken from the courtroom. How much more would I suffer at her hand? How many more times would she go out of her way to hurt me? I couldn't understand it, and at that moment, I was too angry to think about it.

As I was taken from the courtroom, I didn't think about my record deal, or about losing my thuggish girlfriend who had already cheated on me. I was sure she would again. The only thing I could think about was being forced to leave my mama. In that instance, I hated Vickie. Everything was her fault. Had she really traveled hundreds of miles to make sure I went to jail? Did she hate me that much? I felt like my life was spiraling out of control, and I started thinking about ways to stop it. The only solution that came to mind was having a family and living the Christian life I had been raised to have and had seen my foster parents live. I wanted stability, and this looked like the way to get it. All I had to do now was survive the next 360 days.

Vickie, age 2.

Vickie's mother, Maurice's grandmother, Mrs. Mattie Lee McBride.

Vickie's father and Maurice's grandfather, Mr. Thomas McBride.

Vickie, age 7.

The family home on Doyle Street (later renamed Martin Luther King, Jr. Drive) in Waynesboro, GA.

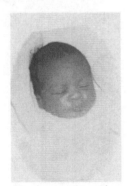

Maurice, two days old.

Maurice, age 2.

Vickie's high school year-book photo.

Photo of Maurice taken at Ben-brook's Five & Dime when Vickie got her first paycheck.

Article about Maurice surviving viral meningitis. (Source: The True Citizen)

Vickie in the Miss Georgia Southern College pageant, freshman year. She was the only Black contestant. (Source: The True Citizen)

Building where Maurice went to day-care.

Maurice, 4th grade.

Vickie (bride) and Maurice (ring bearer) at her first wedding.

At Vickie's graduation from Savannah State College: (from left) Jon, Vickie, Aunt Sammie Joe, Maurice and Uncle Alexander.

Maurice, 7th grade.

Maurice, 10th grade.

Vickie after earning her master's degree from North Carolina Central University.

Maurice (rear) waiting for the subway in New York.

Maurice's identification photo at the Twin City Detention Camp.

MC MOO

Promotional picture taken when Maurice got his record deal with EMI/Capitol Records..

The CD cover for Maurice's single, 2D Frutti. Courtesy of EMI/Capitol Records.

Vickie and Maurice at his master's degree commencement exercise from American InterContinental University.

Maurice's Burke County mug shot.

Maurice (right) and his business partner, Kendrick Bradley, in front of their hair and nail salon.

Da Barnyard Click from left: M.C. Moo (Maurice McBride), Mizz Buttaworf (Tina Hampton), Big Hurk (Torez Green), Darius (Chicken Weezy), and Tyrese (in front).

Rappers Lil' Jon (left) and M.C. Moo (Maurice).

Da Barnyard Click from left: Plug (Kenyotta Burns), M.C. Moo (Maurice McBride), Skare Krow; NKA Flame Beats (Joseph Terry), and Fishbone (Mike Terry)

Maurice and Jessica with Oliver Vance (middle) at a book signing event at Books-a-Million in Talla-hassee, Florida.

Cover of *Oliver Vance, Pull Up Your Pants!*, the children's book written by Maurice McBride and Jessica Wallace McBride.

Maurice and Vickie after the Capella University commencement ceremony in Minneapolis, Minnesota on August 10, 2013.

Dr. Vickie McBride and Dr. Maurice McBride.

Chapter 7
I Got Your Baby!

Vickie

Raising two children alone was tough. Even with a degree, I sometimes struggled financially, but I didn't have time to sit and cry about it. Keeping two growing boys clothed, fed, and protected required that I do whatever it took. Since my mother and aunt were my examples, I knew that more education was my way to financial freedom, so I continued to pursue a master's degree. My enrollment was sporadic, but I wasn't giving up.

I had always planned to raise my family with my husband, yet here I was, trying to bring up two boys on my own. My father had died when I was four years old, and my mother never married again. When I asked her why, she said it was because she didn't want to risk anybody coming into the house and "bothering" me. Later, I realized that she was protecting me from the kind of harm I still ended up enduring at Aunt Sammie Joe's home as a 13-year-old.

As an adopted child, I wanted to create a strong family unit that would stick together. I found out I was adopted from Sherry and Gail Barber, two girls who teased me about it almost every day as I walked home from school. One day when I was about ten years old, I asked, "Mama, what does 'adopted' mean?"

"Where did you hear that?" she inquired.

"Every day when I'm walking home, Sherry and Gail always tell me I'm adopted. What does that mean?"

Without hesitating, she said, "The next time they say that to you, you tell them it means I take better care of you than their mama does them." And that's exactly what I did. By the time I made it home the next day after defining adoption for Sherry and Gail, their grandmother had called my mother to tell her what I said. I'm sure their grandmother thought it would get me in trouble, but she was wrong.

"It's the truth," I heard my mother tell her. "They didn't have any business telling her that anyway." I didn't hear anything from Sherry and Gail about being adopted after that.

Mama did explain adoption a little further at that time, and when I turned 18, she broached the subject again. She explained that although she wasn't the mother who had given birth to me, she was the mother who cared for me. it never bothered me because I knew my mama loved me dearly. Nevertheless, she asked me if I wanted to find my birth mother.

"No," I told her. "You're the only mother I know and the only one I want to know." That feeling never changed. However, since my children are grown and having children of their own, they have asked me to find out more about my birth parents, primarily for medical reasons. I've agreed to do so, but I'm not in any real hurry to do it.

Even though I hadn't had much time with my father before he died, I wanted my boys to have a father in their lives. It wasn't a realistic option to expect Phillip to be active in Maurice's life since he was still denying that Maurice was his. My mother and I had accepted full responsibility for Maurice from the day I brought him home from Louisville, so we never asked that family for anything.

Jon's dad, Desmond, had a good relationship with Maurice, but he had gone to Germany when Jon was only eight months old, and Maurice had only visited on the weekends and during the summer while we dated and were married. Desmond always wanted Maurice to live with us permanently. He could see how much worse his behavior was getting, and thought that living with us would be the best thing for him, but Mama wasn't having it. As I stated, the bond she and Maurice shared was strong.

Maurice loved, yet competed with his brother, Jon. Since I had raised Jon without my mother's interference, we had a different relationship and a clear understanding of our roles in each other's lives. I was the mother, he was the child. I gave directions, he followed them. On the other hand, I was always re-establishing my authority with Maurice. Although we did many fun things together in those early years when I still lived at home, I never thought of myself as nor wanted to be his sister or his friend, only his mother.

86

Since he was raised in a home where we both had to do what Mama said, I imagine that it was the exact opposite for Maurice. To him, I felt like a sister and a friend. The fact that I was his mother was just a technicality.

After our divorce, Desmond remained active in Jon's life, but not Maurice's. He would come to my house and pick up his son so they could spend time together, and Maurice was left behind. It seems obvious now, but I didn't know how painful this was for Maurice at the time. He was well into his adulthood before he ever mentioned this to me. Even if I had known, I don't know that there would have been anything I could have done about it, but it hurts me to know that he was hurting.

When Jon was gone with his dad, I sometimes planned activities with Maurice. I hoped these times would be good for us and help us establish our relationship and build our bond, but Mama's interference prevented those times from being any different. If Maurice couldn't get what he wanted from me and could get to a phone, he would call Mama and there would always be an argument. For years, in fact, I was an authorized user on Mama's Macy's department store account, and she wanted me to use it to buy Maurice the clothes and shoes he needed, and I could use it to buy things for Jon, as well. Even though she didn't place a limit on my spending, I limited it because I knew she was on a fixed income and there was no need to increase her debt unnecessarily. So when Maurice asked for hundred-dollar sneakers, I said no.

"Well, Vickie, if that's what he wants, why didn't you get them?" my mother asked me when he called her.

"Those shoes are too expensive," I answered, "and he doesn't take care of them."

"Well, if that's what he wants, go ahead and get them," she told me. I lost this battle and every one like it. Nevertheless, I wouldn't take advantage of her, so I restricted what I spent on Jon and me. And, whether my mother agreed or not, I was going to punish Maurice for his misbehavior because I was responsible for raising this child, not her.

Try as I might to establish and enforce rules, awful things were happening between Maurice and me, and I tried my best to handle them at home without making the problem public. Even when I went to work with scratches and bruises from Maurice, I ignored my supervisor's advice to get help. One of the scariest times was when Maurice locked himself and Jon in the bedroom they shared. When I tried to get in, he wouldn't unlock the door.

"I have a knife in here with your babyyyy!" he taunted me. Jon was crying and screaming. I had no idea what was happening or why.

"Maurice, open this door! Please open this door!" I begged. I tried to stay calm, but I had not been this scared in a long time. Maurice and I fought, but there were never any weapons involved. And no matter what happened between Maurice and me, I never believed Jon was in any danger. But here I was, standing outside a locked bedroom door listening to my baby scream for me while being held hostage at knifepoint by his brother.

"No!" Maurice yelled. "I got your baby and I have a knife!"

"Jon, come to the door and unlock it," I said. I tried to speak calmly, but he must have heard the fear in my voice, because his screaming and crying got worse.

"He can't come to the door right now," Maurice answered.

After more pleading and being ignored, I called the police. I didn't want to because we lived in one of the nicer apartment communities and I was embarrassed to be "that family" that had the police being called to its home for a domestic incident. I didn't know it then, but this would be the first of many times that I had to involve the authorities over the years, even into Maurice's adulthood. The details of what they said to him that night are a blur, but the police were able to coax him into opening the door, and both he and Jon were unharmed.

To say I was frightened is an understatement. I was shaken to my core. If I was in denial about it before, it became obvious to me at that point that I needed help managing Maurice's behavior. Still, I hesitated. Even now, when Maurice did everything but threaten to kill his brother, I was reluctant to seek help. I wanted to be able to help my child without getting the system involved, but I was being backed into a corner.

As a result of calling the police, the complex would not renew my lease once it ended. The same company owned another apartment community that wasn't nearly as nice, and they allowed us to move in there. I chose to do so instead of finding an apartment owned by a different leasing company because the cheaper rent would relieve some pressure. Despite my college education, the professional experience I was gaining, and the money I earned, I wasn't able to provide the type of lifestyle I wanted for my family because of Maurice's severe behavior problems. I even spent one winter without a coat to make sure my sons had warm clothes, food, and shelter. Nothing in my upbringing or formal training had prepared me for such issues. I was frustrated and confused.

Another incident occurred when Maurice spent the summer before his fifth grade school year in Savannah with Jon and me. We had been living in the other apartment complex for a couple of months when I received a phone call from the police while I was at work one day, explaining that my apartment had been searched and evacuated. This seemed impossible. Maurice had been given strict instructions not to ever let anyone in while I wasn't home, so how could my apartment need to be "evacuated?" As it turned out, Maurice had found my ex-husband's pornography collection and decided to hold a public viewing for the neighborhood boys. I had completely forgotten that the movies even existed, and I have no idea how he found them. After explaining to the police that the movies weren't mine, I hung up and headed home. There was a business card from an officer requesting that I call him. For the second time that day, I spoke to the police about a group of boys viewing pornography in my home. To make matters worse, someone had stolen some of my jewelry from my bedroom. I was *furious.*

I tried talking to Maurice about what happened, but he denied everything. That infuriated me, and I beat him. I was so *angry.* Because of the previous incident involving Maurice, I had been forced to move from a very nice apartment complex into a less desirable one, and now I had been disobeyed again. To add insult to injury, this time I had been robbed. The disrespect and violation cut so deeply that I couldn't see straight. So Maurice didn't get a spanking or get grounded; I b*eat* him. It was probably one of the worst beatings he ever got from me.

At the end of that summer, Maurice returned to Waynesboro, but before the first semester of fifth grade was over, he was back with me because, as I explained before, he had started hanging out all night, sometimes not coming home until three or four in the morning. After a phone call from my mother who was at her wit's end, I drove to Waynesboro and brought him back to Savannah to live with me. His behavior didn't improve at all; we were at constant odds, and our disputes usually turned physical.

I sought individual counseling for Maurice, and family counseling for all of us. Whenever Maurice hit me, I stopped seeing him as my son and only saw him as a man. He was taller than me by then, but truthfully, that had very little to do with it. After being raped as a young teen, I decided that any man that raised his hand against me was going to be in for the fight of his life. I wasn't just fighting a physical battle; I was fighting against powerlessness and victimization.

At the end of another fight with Maurice, I had bruises and a busted lip. When I went to work, my supervisor, who was also my friend, sat me down and said, "Enough is enough. You cannot allow this child to do this to you anymore." I broke down and cried. She was right; I couldn't deny it any longer, and I couldn't protect him from harsher consequences anymore, so I agreed to get help. I knew exactly what happened to black boys with his temper and defiant attitude, and although I had been hurt by him, I was afraid of what would be done to him in the long run in a society that thought so poorly of black boys and placed so little value on their lives. Still, I hesitated.

Maurice went back to Waynesboro for sixth grade, but didn't make it through the school year. He left campus and refused to return, so the principal wouldn't allow him back in school. When Mama called me, I called Charter Savannah Behavioral Health for help. I had to seek some sort of intervention for Maurice because, at the rate we were going when we lived together, one of us was going to die, and it wasn't going to be me. I felt frustrated, confused, and helpless. Charter was a local facility that offered behavioral programs for children. After speaking with a counselor there, I decided that their behavior modification program was the best option for Maurice.

I picked Maurice up from Waynesboro again, and when we arrived in Savannah, I told him he had to admit himself to Charter because he needed help that I couldn't provide. I didn't want to send him there, and he didn't want to go, but I didn't know what else to do. His little brother, Jon, was with me when I dropped him off there the next day. We all cried. I felt like a failure as a parent, but I prayed that this intervention would do the trick. My mother was extremely upset when she found out and tried to negotiate with me and bribe me to change my mind, but there was nothing she could say or do. She couldn't handle him, and at this point, neither could I.

Maurice stayed at Charter treatment center for 30 days at a cost of $14,000. Since it wasn't covered by my ex-husband's military medical insurance, I had to pay for it out of pocket, and it took me several years to do so. During his time at Charter, we had weekly family counseling and there were more tears. I could tell that my child was hurting and Jon and I were hurting along with him. I prayed and prayed that his stay there would make the difference. At one of the sessions, Maurice gave me a jewelry box he'd made for me. I still have that jewelry box today.

As the end of the 30-day term approached, the counselors at the treatment center started talking to me about the next move. They diagnosed Maurice with Oppositional Defiant Disorder and recommended long-term care and medication. I couldn't do it. Although Maurice still had behavior problems, even while in the treatment program, I chose to bring him home. I didn't know if anything had really changed, but he promised to do better, and I felt so bad about him being there that I couldn't make him stay any longer. He really hated being in the treatment center, and I hoped that the threat of having to go there again would keep him on the straight and narrow. It did - for about two weeks. Slowly, the old behaviors returned and within a few weeks, I was dealing with the same defiant, disrespectful, manipulative adolescent. I couldn't see where his time there or the money spent had made a significant difference.

No matter what was going on at home, I never had to go to Maurice's school the entire time we lived in Savannah. I can't say that about any other place we lived. He always performed well academically, but his behavior was a constant problem in other cities. We moved a couple of times so that I could take advantage of better opportunities for my family, but most of the time we moved because Maurice's behavior problems at school or misconduct in the community prompted it. Each time we relocated, I hoped the new city or state would mean something better for him, but it didn't. The behaviors were the same no matter where we lived. Eventually, I had to admit that it wasn't the environment that needed to change, it was the child.

Things got so bad with Maurice that sometimes, I just put him out of the house. He caused such a huge disruption, and the tension between him and my fiancé, Larry, always ended in an uproar. I didn't marry Larry because I could never bring myself to set a date. Something about him just wasn't right. Well, that "something" turned out to be "someone;" I discovered that I wasn't his only fiancé. Thank God I dodged that bullet.

Eventually, we moved to Warner Robins, Georgia, where I continued working for the Department of Defense. I always hoped a new city and new friends would mean a new start for Maurice, but it never did. Things were terrible between him and me. His defiance, verbal and physical aggression, and complete disregard for my authority and anyone else's were making our lives a living hell. It soon became clear, however, that I was grossly underestimating the level of intelligence and manipulation Maurice had. For instance, anytime he was grounded and forbidden to leave the house, he would engage me in an argument and then storm out. Even when I picked up on this pattern, I was unable to prevent the behavior. I could see it coming, but I didn't have the skills to stop it. Sometimes I didn't allow him back into the apartment when he did this in hopes that the possibility of being locked out would stop him, but it never did.

Every time there was a problem, Maurice called Mama, and she called me. On one occasion when I wouldn't talk to her, she called social services and Maurice's relationship with the foster care system began. Maurice moved in and out of several different foster homes over the next few years. His longest stay came after a judge put him in foster care following repeated stays at YDC and because he would not abide by my rules. The court date and decision came on the heels of an incident where Maurice broke curfew, again, and I wouldn't let him in my house. When the police arrived with him in tow, I told them that all of my children follow my rules, and no child of mine was out after 11:00 pm. They took him to YDC where he stayed as he awaited our court date.

My mother came to court but wasn't allowed to speak. She wanted to take Maurice with her back to Waynesboro, but the judge didn't permit her to do so because of Maurice's track record and Mama's age. Once I explained that Maurice was defiant and incorrigible, and refused to follow my rules, the judge placed him in foster care for 30 days. I wasn't happy about this, but it was better than having him destroy our home, and it was better than having him at Charter treatment center. Again, I hoped this would change his course, but it didn't. He wreaked havoc in the foster homes. When he came home for special occasions, however, we got along okay.

Eventually, Maurice came back home, but this pattern would repeat itself several times. He would act out, we would fight, the police would come, and he would be placed in foster care. The last straw was when he hit me in the eye. As much as I tried to shield Jon from this drama, he witnessed much of this conflict. As children sometimes do, Jon blurted out to my supervisor one morning that "my brother hit my mama in the eye." My supervisor reported it and took pictures of my injury. This led to another court date, and when the judge saw pictures of my black eye in court, Maurice was sent to foster care with the threat of detention. My mother asked for him to be allowed to live with her and was again denied. Needless to say, Maurice ended up in detention. Again, he came home for visits, and when Jon and I moved to Beaufort, South Carolina, Maurice came with us. We moved to a new city in a new state, but Maurice had the same problems.

After being told not to leave the house one day while I was gone, Maurice left anyway. While he and some friends were walking a girl home at dusk, he was attacked, beaten, and burned with cigarettes. I came home to a bruised and swollen child. I was angry at him for going out, but I was more angry at whomever had hurt him. I took him to the emergency room and filed a police report. Maurice knew who had attacked him so we pressed charges, went to court, and won. I hoped that this incident would curb some of his negative behaviors, but it didn't. The wounds healed and he kept doing what he wanted to do.

By this time, I was pregnant with my third child from my second husband, Ethan, and we were living in Sumter, South Carolina. I held a different position, but I was still working for the Department of Defense. If there was ever a marriage I regretted, it was this one. I had ended the relationship with Ethan before moving to Sumter, but gave him another chance when I found out I was pregnant. In October of 1991, I gave birth to my daughter whom I named Avia, and I married Ethan shortly afterwards. As I stated before, I wanted my children to have their fathers in their lives, and I never wanted to live with a man I wasn't married to because I thought that set a bad example. Looking back, that would have been preferable to the five horrible years I put my children through during my relationship with Ethan.

I ignored numerous red flags when we dated, the most glaring of which was my son Jon's reaction when I told him that Ethan and I were getting married. He broke down in tears.

"Please don't marry him, Mama!" he sobbed. I was completely caught off guard. Maurice had been about Jon's age when I married Desmond, and he had not reacted this way. In fact, he had been excited.

"Why, baby?" I asked Jon.

"I don't want you to marry him! Please, Mama! Please don't marry him!" Jon begged. My children were used to having me all to themselves, so I figured Jon's reaction was related this.

"It's going to be alright," I told him. I was wrong.

Ethan was just a sorry man with some low down behaviors. He lied, he robbed change machines, tried to teach my sons illegal things, had sex with underage girls, and never wanted to see me do well. I was trying to earn my master's degree at the time, and he would wait until the last minute, then refuse to watch the children in an attempt to keep me from going to class. Strangely, Ethan and Maurice resembled each other quite a bit, and Ethan sometimes used Maurice's name when he did dirt, which led to Maurice being accused of doing things Ethan had actually done. Once, a woman came to my home and told me that if she caught Maurice in her house with her daughters again, she would call the police. Well, Maurice had been at home with me the entire time. It was actually Ethan who had been with her daughters.

Ethan verbally berated the children all the time, but never physically abused them. I can't say the same for his behavior toward me; we fought regularly. My children knew the routine when a fight started between Ethan and me. They would go to the car and stay there until I said it was safe to come back into the house. Maurice always wanted to defend me against Ethan because, even though Maurice and I fought, he wouldn't stand by and let anyone else hurt me. I knew that allowing Maurice to intervene could lead to something much worse than scratches and bruises, so I always tried to prevent that.

Ethan was abusive, but he got as good as he gave. As I said before, no man was going to hurt me or violate me without me defending myself. After one of our worst fights, I pressed charges against him and we had to go to court. Ethan tried to convince me not to testify against him, but it didn't work. He was fined $500 and would have to do time if the physical abuse happened again. The threat of incarceration worked, but the other forms of abuse and disrespect continued.

Over the course of the marriage, I got pregnant a second time. I loved my children, but I was devastated when I discovered I was pregnant again from this horrible man. Maurice and Jon were eight years apart, and Avia was eight years younger than Jon, so having another baby while Avia was still in diapers was something I couldn't fathom. I was in an unstable relationship with an abusive, mean-spirited, deceitful man who had shown me time and time again that he would never change. I was struggling to raise three children practically on my own and couldn't imagine myself raising four, so I planned to end the pregnancy. I prayed for peace about the decision to abort, but it never came.

Still, I planned to go through with it. Ethan and I went to the abortion clinic together. As we waited for my name to be called, I tried to come to terms with this choice. I clasped my hands in my lap, closed my eyes, and prayed. I knew this wasn't what God would want, but I pleaded to Him anyway, begging Him to end the turmoil I felt in my spirit about this decision. He finally spoke to me.

"Man of God."

What? I wondered. I stilled, kept my eyes closed, and listened.

"Man of God," I heard again. That was all the confirmation I needed. This child I was carrying was special and would grow to be a man of God. There was no way I could terminate this pregnancy, no matter what circumstances I faced. I released the breath I didn't know I had been holding, opened my eyes, and looked at Ethan.

"Let's go get something to eat," I told him.

He stared back at me. "Are you sure?" he asked.

"Yeah, let's go get something to eat," I repeated. We left the abortion clinic that day and I have never regretted that decision.

I gave birth to my fourth child in March of 1993. This one was a boy whom I named after his father but call by his middle name, Brien. On the day I brought Brien home from the hospital, I received a phone call from one of the mothers of Ethan's other children. When I'd met Ethan, he had no children, and he swore that the two women claiming to be pregnant from him (one of whom was married, the other of whom was just 15 years old) were lying. I didn't believe him, but his sister convinced me that he was being honest, so I remained in a relationship with him. By the time Avia was born, I had learned that both women had been telling the truth and had given birth about one month apart. Yet, as I held Brien in one arm and the phone in the opposite hand, I was still shocked by what I was hearing.

"I know you just got home from the hospital and I don't mean to disrespect you," the married one said after we greeted each other, "but I need to speak to Ethan about our children."

When Ethan and I got married, I told both of the other women who had his children that they could call anytime because Ethan needed to be a responsible father to all of his kids, so her phone call wasn't a problem. Her wanting to talk about their *children* instead of their *child* was.

I looked at Ethan and kept talking to her. "What children?"

"Don't listen to her!" he interjected. "Let me talk to her."

"No," I told him. "What children?" I asked her again. He could only sit and stare as the story unfolded.

"He didn't tell you?" she said.

"Tell me what?"

"We have another baby together," she told me.

I took a deep breath. "Another baby? How old is it?"

"I had her about a month after you had Avia," she told me. "I can't believe he didn't tell you."

I handed Ethan the phone, sat down on the couch with Brien in my arms, and cried. I just couldn't believe it. It wasn't that I expected something better from him; I was simply overwhelmed by the enormity of the task I faced as the mother of a toddler and a newborn from this lying, cheating, no-good man. My emotions were all over the place, and the feelings of hurt and betrayal quickly turned to rage. I made the decision I should have made years before. I got up from the sofa, placed Brien in his crib, and stared at Ethan.

"Get out!" I screamed at him. "Get the hell out of my house and don't bring your sorry ass back!" He tried to talk to me, of course, but I refused to listen. I could accept children from before we were married, but this was just too much. I yelled and cursed until he left with a few belongings in hand.

Over the next few months, Ethan was relentless in his efforts to talk his way back into my life. He called constantly and came around "to see the kids" often, no matter what I said. I suppose I was vulnerable - not because of any love I had for him, but because I wanted my children to have their father in their lives, even one as awful as him.

"We need to raise our children together," he told me repeatedly. He knew that was important to me, and he used it to worm his way back into my life. We didn't work anything out or resolve any issues; he just came back. Once he was back in, it wasn't long before he confirmed what I already knew: He hadn't changed and never would.

What ended the cycle for me was when Brien's babysitter told me I had to get out of the relationship because it was harming my children. I knew that, but for some reason, hearing it from her made it real. For me, that was *the end*. Following the advice I'd heard Oprah Winfrey give to women who needed to get out of bad situations, I started putting my exit plan into action. It took a couple of years to secure myself and my children so that I could get away from Ethan. Eventually, I found a house for rent across the street from the babysitter. As my departure date got closer, I even borrowed money from a friend who always said she would help whenever I was ready to leave. She had one stipulation, though: If I went back to Ethan, I'd have to pay her back immediately. I gave her my word and finally left Ethan for good. After two children and five years of his lying, cheating, stealing, and verbal and physical abuse, I filed for divorce and I never looked back. I later apologized to my children for subjecting them to such a terrible environment. It is one of my deepest regrets.

Now I was a single mother of four. I had finally acquiesced to Mama's rant and allowed Maurice to return to Waynesboro. I was tired of the battle that I had been fighting with her all of his life. I should have taken him when Desmond said to do so years before, but I hadn't. When I sent him back, I told her not to tell me anything about the problems I was sure he would continue to have. That didn't stop her from calling constantly to tell me what he was doing. I intervened very little, because I knew better than to believe that anything I said over the phone would make a difference. Maurice was about 15 by now, and although my brother Don tried to step in as his behavior worsened, it was too late.

The battle over Maurice had permanently damaged my relationship with my mother, but once he was out of my house, my relationship with him improved because I wasn't in direct authority over him. Our interaction was limited to family trips and vacations, so the potential for conflict was diminished. I still worried, though, and just prayed that he would at least graduate from high school. When he dropped out during his second year of tenth grade, I thought all hope was lost. Thank God I was wrong.

Chapter 8
Lockup: Twin City

Maurice

Over the years, I have talked openly about my troubled youth and the time I spent in jail. It's a regrettable but important part of my past, and I always hope that talking about it will help someone avoid it, or help an ex-offender get on the right path.

At some point during our courtship, my wife Jessica asked me, "Why did you have to go to jail so much? Wasn't once enough? Why did you have to keep doing stuff until you got the long sentence?"

I answered her honestly. "Jail wasn't that bad," I told her. "The county jail was always full of people I knew. I always had friends in county jail; it was almost like school. If I ran out of money, my friends shared what they had. Sometimes, that doesn't even happen on the streets. Being locked up really wasn't that bad."

That was true until the judge sentenced me to 360 days in the Emanuel Probation Detention Center for my most recent probation violation. I was in the county jail for a month, and then I was transported to the military-style camp in Twin City. While I waited to be transported, I was constantly on the phone with my lawyer, trying to get into a program to avoid the detention center, but it didn't happen. In fact, nothing that I tried worked. I had been able to manipulate the system in my favor every time before, but this time was different. To say I was distraught was an understatement. I was 19 years old, and I couldn't skate by on my mama's reputation and money anymore.

I was taken to the work camp in the same suit I had worn to court. Once there, I was ordered to strip, and my head was shaved, and I was issued an orange jumpsuit. After a medical check-up, the other offenders and I were told what we would do and would not do. All of the bravado and defiance that had ruled my life before had been replaced by depression and defeat. Unlike the county jail, I knew only one person in this place, and he was on his way home.

He introduced me to some people and kind of vouched for me before he left, but that was it. I was on my own. Inmates unofficially formed groups based on where they were from, but I was the only one there from Waynesboro, so I hung with the Christian group. I was only about 40 miles away from home, but since Mama was sick and elderly, and I doubted that Vickie and my siblings would visit from North Carolina, it might as well have been 400 miles.

Everyone at the detention center had much shorter sentences than I did, and I met some interesting characters there. One was a lawyer, which was a total shock to me. Not only was he on the wrong side of the law, he was in a detention camp, not a comfortable, low-security prison. I also encountered a person with Parkinson's disease for the first time. His name was Mr. Pruitt. I had no idea what it was, so as I talked to Mr. Pruitt about my case, I felt like he was giving me mixed messages when he responded.

"So what do you think, Mr. Pruitt? Do I have a good chance of getting out?" I asked him after sharing the details of my criminal history.

"Yeah, I think you have a pretty good chance," he said. But he was shaking his head no. I didn't know what to make of it. Was he just saying yes to make me feel better? I was confused until I learned from another inmate that Mr. Pruitt had Parkinson's disease and couldn't control the shaking.

Homosexuality, which I hadn't encountered at the county jail, ran rampant in the detention camp. The inmates' favorite was a man we called Red. I would often hear men comment on Red's figure as though he were a woman, and I was bewildered. Red was clearly male, and no matter how he talked or walked, that's all I saw when I looked at him. Even the inmates I would have never suspected would do anything like that eventually played in the Red zone. Their behavior made me decide to sleep propped up on the top bunk, on my back. I stayed awake until everyone else had gone to sleep. I always showered alone, which meant I went to the showers much earlier or much later than everyone else. The only thing Red could do for me was take a letter to my girlfriend when he got out, which he did.

Strangely, I met a lot of inmates with missing eyes. It's not that a missing eye was new to me, but I had never been around so many people at once who had missing eyes. I hoped that they had come there with them already missing and hadn't lost them at the camp. Leaving Twin City with both of my eyes and my manhood intact became my primary goals.

The Bible was always present when I was locked up. Honestly, the only time I read the Bible was when I was in jail. I would get out and try to live a Christian life, but the pull of the streets was too strong. It was only a matter of time before I was back to my old habits. Nevertheless, I was determined that this time would be different. I didn't want to be here, and I was starting to see the pattern: Do something bad, get locked up. I had to break the cycle, and the only thing I knew to do was try to live according to the good book. So I prayed, read the Bible, and went to the church services they offered. I stayed in my own space and didn't interact too much with other inmates unless they were much older. I avoided all of the foolishness that can extend your time behind bars because I was always trying to figure out how to get out. Still, there were problems.

We had to do the most difficult, back-breaking work at that camp. For at least eight hours a day, we shoveled human waste at the water treatment plant, broke beaver dams, cut dozens of acres of grass with push lawnmowers, picked up trash on county roads and at the dump, and laid asphalt. Vickie's words rang in my ears every time I stood ankle-deep in human excrement. Each time I had gotten in trouble, she had warned, "Keep on, and you'll be in jail shoveling shit." I had no idea she meant that literally. I had never even seen a beaver dam before, yet there I was, knee-deep in a river inhabited by water moccasins, swinging a bush ax to destroy what the beavers had worked so hard to build. Picking up trash at the dump was the most useless labor of all. We walked in a circle around a mountain of garbage, filling our plastic bags with discarded things, many of them unrecognizable. Once a bag was full, we tied it up and threw it on top of the trash heap. It was a colossal waste of time and energy, but any complaints were ignored or punished, and the punishments were harsher for blacks.

One day, I was pushed to the edge by the heat, disrespect, and exhaustion. When one of the officers said something derogatory to me, I blew up.

"Man, this is modern day slavery!" I yelled. I wasn't expecting a response, but I got one. It came from the other detainees.

"Yeah!" they said. "You right!" That gave me some fire. I didn't know how far they were willing to take it, but there was only one way to find out. After taking one look at us and feeling the shift in the atmosphere, the officer immediately called for backup.

"We don't have to take this!" I continued. "Let's buck the system and go home. It's 15 of us and only one of him!" I could see that they were ready to act, and although I thought about escaping all the time, I didn't have a plan. Backup arrived quickly and that uprising was over before it started. That outburst earned me seven days in solitary confinement with horrible food and showers only every other day. I hated being there, but at least I didn't have to sleep with one eye open. On the seventh day, the detention camp's phone bill arrived and they discovered that I had been sneaking into the guards' office to make long distance calls to my girlfriend. That earned me 14 more days in the hole.

I could have saved myself the trouble because my girlfriend didn't stand by me. On the streets, she had been my ride-or-die chick, doing things like loading bullets in my gun and jumping in if I got in a fight. She had even bailed me out once. Soon after I arrived at the detention center, the daily letters I had been receiving from her started coming weekly, then monthly, then not at all. My birthday came and went without even getting a card from her. She promised to visit but never did. The only person who did visit was Vickie. I was happy to see her both times that she came, but there was also some resentment because I believed she had testified against me to get me locked up. On her first visit, she brought my brother Jon. I was happy to see him, but the visit was tense.

The second visit was emotional. As I sat in the visitation area and talked to her, I broke down in tears. I was afraid, not of being locked up, but of getting out and not being able to avoid coming back again. I just wasn't sure I could do it. She gave me the standard advice about doing the right thing, staying away from the wrong people, etc. I hoped and prayed that I could. My bad decisions had already caused me to spend too many special days locked up, and the attitudes of correctional officers didn't change just because it was an inmate's birthday or because there was a holiday. In addition to the weekly phone call each inmate was allowed to make, one extra phone call was permitted on our birthdays, and Thanksgiving was celebrated with something that remotely resembled turkey covered in a liquid that was supposed to be gravy. On Christmas day, we were lined up and each given the same thing: a small brown paper bag filled with unshelled pecans and individually wrapped peppermints. "Merry Christmas," the guard said stoically each time he handed an inmate his "gift." On that day, I saw the toughest detainees shed tears, and I learned that you don't have to have eyes to cry as tears ran from occupied sockets and empty ones.

I missed my mama tremendously. I was worried about her because she was in her 80's by now and was having health problems. Nevertheless, she was always working on getting me home. She was in constant communication with my lawyer, and she always sent money and letters. I felt very guilty for letting her down and made a commitment to myself to be better. To keep her phone bill low, I would call one of my aunts and she would call my mama for me using a three-way calling feature. Mama was paying for my lawyer; she shouldn't have to pay a high phone bill, too.

Reading the Bible in jail started me on a path of forgiveness toward my mother, my father, and so many others who had hurt me. It didn't happen overnight, but the wounds started to heal, although there are still scars that tell the tale. I also read *Popular Science* and financial magazines, like *Business Week*. I went to the Emanuel Probation Detention Center as a wild teenager, but I felt like I came out a man. I hated being locked up and actually could have escaped several times, but reading the Bible led me to make a different choice. It also helped me formulate a plan for doing things differently when I got out.

I hated the food they served us in Twin City, so I kept a locker full of candy and snacks. One day, I shared my stash with a friend who was hungry. As I stared at the candy and snacks, my dormant creativity began to awaken, and I started freestyle rapping about my commissary. I liked what I was thinking, so I wrote down what would become the first verse of "2D Frutti," my Billboard Top Ten single. I asked my friend to write the second verse. I thought about the days when New Edition inspired me to put together a singing group, but we always ended up playing. I wasn't playing anymore. So, when he said no to my invitation and chose to play basketball instead of creating a song, that didn't stop me. I stayed in my cell and kept writing.

I liked what I had started and decided to keep going. My love for music had not dissipated, and my re-emerging creativity needed an outlet. Over a period of days, I wrote the hook and refined the first verse. My friend liked it, but the other inmates dissed it. Gangsta rap was ruling the airways, and they didn't think my song about candy and snacks could compete with the "thug life" being perpetuated through music. Their discouragement only fueled my determination to do something unique.

Soon after Vickie's second visit, I got released. I had served 240 days instead of 360, and felt blessed to be a free man. I was feeling hopeful and confident that I could stick to my plan and avoid being locked up again. Not everyone shared my optimism. As I was leaving the facility, my counselor said to me, "You'll be back."

I paused and looked at her. She was a young white female who had never provided any real support to me. I imagined how her experience in corrections might have lead her to believe that all inmates re-offended, which made her the worst kind of person to be assigned to assist with rehabilitation. I could have ignored her or cursed her out, but instead, I told her, "God bless you, too, and you'll be locked up here before I will." She didn't respond.

When I made it home, Mama was so happy to see me, and I was ecstatic to see her, but I could see that the eight months without me had taken its toll. I was determined to do things right this time so that I wouldn't have to be away from her for that long

105

again, so I got a job at McDonald's because working was a condition of my release, and I read the Bible and prayed every day. Yet, the relief from deprivation and my newfound freedom led me to make a few bad decisions once I was released. There were some close calls, and a couple of police chases that my friends still talk about, but luckily, I wasn't arrested for any serious parole violations.

The song I had started writing was still in my head and on my heart, so when I saw a member of Duice, I told him about it. Then I went to see my friend Tony Jackson who had just come home from the military. Tony's nickname is Groove, and he had a keyboard in an old tin shed on his family's lot in Keysville, a few miles from Waynesboro. He produced a beat for my verse and I practiced it over and over, but somehow, he lost it. Since Groove is so talented, he created another beat and even convinced a friend of ours, Tim Jeffers, to sing the hook. I was glad, because after my experience with Aunt Sammie Joe's dog, Jo-Jo, I knew it was best if I didn't do it. Hearing Tim sing the hook inspired me, and later that night on the phone with a girl I liked, I finished writing "2D Frutti." The title came from a flavor of ice cream. I went back to Groove's house the next morning, and we spent the entire day in the tin shed with the keyboard. The next day, we brought the singer in so he could record the hook. I cannot describe how hot it was in that shed. We perspired nonstop; there wasn't even a fan to circulate the stifling air, but we didn't care. Groove's love of music paralleled mine, and we were in a zone. Years later, the recording scenes from the movie *Hustle and Flow* reminded me of those days in the tin shed. We were driven by our commitment to the dream. A little sweat wasn't going to stop us.

I needed time in a real studio, so I asked Mama for the money. McDonald's paid, but not like that. "Go bring me by pocketbook," she said. I couldn't help but smile. She gave me the $300 I needed to go to Beat 0 Studios and record my song. Later that week, Groove, Tim, and I went in and laid down the track.

Tim introduced me to a couple of people starting their own label. They were interested in me, and sent me to a photographer to take promotional pictures. I contacted the photographer and set an

106

appointment. When I arrived, I let him hear my song. He loved it and wanted a copy to share. When I let David "Pressha" Jones hear it, he loved it, too, and asked to be on it. I wasn't sure at first about what he could contribute, but he ended up adding a great intro.

Shortly afterwards, I was offered a $100,000 deal by EMI/Capitol Records. The deal I negotiated required that they pay my mama back the $300. It was a small amount, and she didn't care about it one bit, but it was a way for me to recognize her never-ending support of my dreams. In order for the paperwork to be drawn up, I had to tell them my stage name. Everyone knew me as M.C. Moo, and that wasn't going to change. I needed a way to include everyone who was working with me professionally, so we became Da Barnyard Click featuring M.C. Moo. The group members always changed as aspiring singers, rappers, and producers came and went, but the name remained the same.

Getting that record deal ended the scripture reading and meditation I had been doing, and eventually my life as a rapper pulled my focus in a different direction. The Bible started collecting dust again, and I quit my job at McDonald's. Luckily, I still managed to avoid long jail sentences. I didn't fear extended stay anymore, so I had no fear at all. I knew I could do the time; it wouldn't do me. Nevertheless, I was done with stealing, and stayed away from guns. Now the legal issues I had were mostly related to traffic violations. I spent the occasional night or two in county jail, but I never caught another serious charge. Like too many black males, I experienced racial profiling and challenged the police every time I was stopped unjustly. I still hadn't learned how to pick my battles, and I didn't realize that every battle wasn't worth fighting; I only knew how to fight. I know now that some battles are won silently.

When I actually got the $100,000 check, the phone started ringing off the hook and my mama was happy. Instead of people calling to tell her that I had done something wrong, they called to congratulate her on the wonderful boy she raised. Knowing that I made my mama proud and putting a smile on her face instead of tears in her eyes helped me to forgive myself for all of the pain I had caused her. She saw me on the news doing interviews, and she was proud of me although she didn't fully understand what I was doing.

"Baby, what exactly do you do?" Mama asked me one day.

"I rap," I told her.

"Well what is that? Is it like singing?" she asked.

"Kind of, but not really," I told her. She left it at that.

Of course, Vickie jumped on the bandwagon once I was successful, but I had to get something off of my chest before she could ride. "You were wrong about your son," I told her. Those words were enough to allow me to release the pain I felt for the physical and verbal beatdowns I had taken at her hand. I was still hurt, but I wasn't malicious or stingy, so after I got the "I told you so" out of my system, I said, "Now how much do you need?" That record deal allowed me to be a provider for my mama, Vickie, and my siblings, and I was happy to do it.

Vickie had always told me that being a rapper was a pipe dream that wasn't going to come true. She hadn't thought much of the steps I had taken along this journey - whether it was winning a 4-H competition in 6th grade or being an opening act for other groups, but she had a lot of respect for that six-figure check! While my manager handled big shows, Vickie set up smaller shows and appearances in other states. She was kind of like my road manager. She enjoyed rubbing elbows with stars, and I enjoyed seeing her happy.

We had a rocky relationship, but I loved Vickie. She had been my best friend before she went away to college, and then I had lost that. Still, it made me happy to see her happy, so I didn't have a problem with her reaping a few benefits from my success. At that point, I don't think either one of us guessed that there were even happier moments in our future.

Chapter 9
Separate Vehicles

Vickie

In 1995, I got a job in Cooperative Extension at North Carolina State University as field faculty. I was responsible for educating people in the community about a topic that impacted them, and I chose early childhood education and elder care. The job required a master's degree. Since North Carolina State University was willing to pay for one class per semester at North Carolina Central University, I decided to go for it and began a master's degree program in August 1996. Although I had been taking graduate courses on and off for years (since graduating with my bachelor's degree, in fact), this time I wouldn't stop until I earned it. After taking a couple of classes, I figured out that I could finish the program in two and a half years instead of four by taking two classes at a time, and it wouldn't cost me much more, so that's what I did. This added even more to my plate, but I had three of my four children still in my home, and it was all about securing my future and theirs.

In 1997, I had the opportunity to work from home. As the state specialist for the Child Development Associate Rural Scholarship Program, I trained child care professionals in child development techniques and professionalism in 45 counties. I created my own schedule, and the flexibility allowed more time to complete course requirements for school. Back in Waynesboro, Maurice was caring for Mama who was in her late 80s. By now, he had dropped out of high school, been incarcerated several times, earned his GED, and gotten a record deal. To my surprise, his dream of being a rapper had come true. Honestly, I had never encouraged his interest in music, preferring to direct him along the more secure path of a good education. I believed that being a rapper was a pipe dream and that he should focus on doing well in school and going to college. He proved me wrong. He had a hit song, he could support himself and Mama, and he was generous with me and his siblings. I still wanted him to get a good education, however. He couldn't be a rapper forever.

I enjoyed some of the fringe benefits of his career, like going to parties and meeting performers I admired. Since I was in my early 30s and have always looked younger than I am, my presence didn't cause a problem unless one of Maurice's friends assumed I was his sister instead of his mother and tried to hit on me. He thought it was wrong; I thought it was funny.

Soon after signing his record deal, Maurice wanted me to meet his management team. Even though he was an adult, I remained interested in whoever was playing an important role in my son's life, so I was happy to meet anyone who was working with him. On a trip to Waynesboro, Maurice and I drove to Augusta to have lunch with one of his managers. Imagine my surprise when he introduced me to Tommy, my first "summer love!" The look on Tommy's face was one I will never forget. Even though Maurice and I had the same last name and were from the same town, I guess Tommy had never made the connection and had no idea that Maurice was my son. We greeted each other kindly, and as I stared at Tommy in pleasant surprise, he stared back in shock. It had been almost 20 years since we'd spent that summer together, and I didn't know what he was feeling until he tried to speak.

"Is this…? Maurice is…? Is he my…?" he stammered.

Huh? I thought. Then it hit me. Tommy thought Maurice was his son! I looked at Maurice and the look of growing alarm that spread across his face made me burst out laughing. As the two men stared at me, I assured Tommy that Maurice was not his son and was almost three years old by the time we spent our summer together. He couldn't believe it.

"So you had a son back then?" he asked.

"Yes," I confirmed. He smiled with noticeable relief. Once that worry was gone, the three of us were able to enjoy a pleasant lunch. Maurice didn't like the fact that his manager and his mother had been teenage lovers, but there was nothing he could do about it. He can laugh about it now, but he wasn't laughing then.

110

My relationship with Maurice hadn't healed, but it didn't get any worse. We weren't living together, and he was an adult now. I was thankful for the bond Mama and Maurice shared because I knew he would give her the best possible care. My relationship with her hadn't healed, either, but I loved her and she loved me. That would have to be enough.

In 1998, my second son, Jon, failed ninth grade. He was an easy child to raise and an intelligent boy, but school was a social scene for him where having fun was first and learning was a distant second. That same year, I met David, the man who would become my third husband. Unlike my second husband, he supported my desire for an advanced education and wasn't threatened by it. I needed the support of a partner in order to parent, work, and go to school, so I married David in 1998. He was a nice guy and my children loved him. He had children of his own, and everyone got along like one big happy family. I was working at North Carolina State University, establishing a daycare business, and teaching part time. David's consistent, helpful presence was very valuable.

When Jon failed the first semester of his second year of ninth grade, I decided to home school him. So, when I graduated in December 1999 with a master's degree in Human Development, I created my own curriculum and taught Jon at home for three years. He still had some typical high school experiences, like going to prom, and he started working part time when he turned 16. After completing the requirements to earn a diploma, Jon became a parent at the age of 17. I knew he was sexually active and had warned him that if he got his girlfriend pregnant, he would be present at every doctor's appointment, get her anything she wanted at any time, and always be available to her. I was still shocked when it happened. Not only had I been a young mother, I was now a young grandmother at the age of 39.

Despite David's support and positive presence in my children's lives, turbulence developed in our marriage. One of the major catalysts that led us to divorce happened on a fishing trip one afternoon. David had borrowed my car to go to Virginia one weekend, and when he returned, we piled all of the children into two vehicles to go fishing. He continued to drive my car, and I drove his. For some reason - it may have been because he was speeding - he was stopped by the police on the way home from the fishing trip. A search of the vehicle turned up a glove compartment full of small bags of marijuana. My car was impounded and I had to get it back from the police. Thankfully, they believed me when I told them that the drugs weren't mine and I had no idea how marijuana had gotten in my car. My husband was charged with intent to distribute, a misdemeanor offense.

On another occasion, I found an organizer that belonged to David. He had been looking high and low for it before leaving town on another trip, and I discovered it one day while I was cleaning. It had phone numbers in it, as I expected, but I didn't expect the white powder and razor I found along with the phone numbers, and I didn't expect one of the numbers to be for someone named Kelly in Maryland. She had a star beside her name, so I called. When I identified myself as David's wife and requested to speak to him, he reluctantly came to the phone.

"Look," I told him, "you have five hours to be standing at the foot of my bed, or everything you own will be in ashes." He must have believed me, because Kelly called me back and wanted to know what I had said to make "her man" leave. Clearly, she was delusional. I was the *Mrs.*; she was the *mistress*. I didn't owe her an explanation, so she didn't get one. Instead, I told her that my problem wasn't with her, and encouraged her to lose my number. I had no reason to fight for a man I didn't want to keep.

In less time than I thought was possible, David was standing at the foot of my bed. That saved his belongings, but it didn't keep us together. I had always told him that there were two things that would end our marriage: drugs and infidelity. If he hadn't believed me before, he believed me now. We legally separated, but because of his strong presence in my children's lives and the relationship they had developed with his children, he still lived in the house. It was clear that he had no intention of ever leaving, and was hoping for a reconciliation. To make sure he understood that the marriage was over despite where he slept, I rented a one-room efficiency, and that's where I would spend my nights. After work, my daily routine involved coming home, caring for my children until bed time, leaving around 11 pm to go to my efficiency, and returning in the morning to get them ready for school. He was a sorry husband, but was great with and for the children, and I was reluctant to take that away from them.

We lived this way for a year before I realized that if I didn't push for a divorce, it would never happen. I knew we would never reconcile, and as long as I allowed this living arrangement, nothing would change. I knew what I had to do to give my estranged husband a wakeup call. I started seeing someone else - a much younger someone else. I never wanted a relationship with this person; I just wanted to light a fire under David. Well, that did it. He moved into his parents' home where he still lives. We eventually divorced, but we still maintain the familial atmosphere for the children, even today. Although all of my children are adults, David is still the best father figure they have known.

Throughout these years, I stayed involved in church, and kept the kids involved, too. While living in Savannah, I attended Overcoming by Faith. The pastor, Ricky Temple, explained the real-life application of biblical principles. It was the first time in my life I had been taught in church instead of preached to. I also liked that Overcoming by Faith always had activities for the children. When I lived in North Carolina, I joined another good church, but it became too expensive to attend. They were constantly raising money for something, and they had a way of making you feel uncomfortable if you couldn't contribute. However, they were always willing to help members in need. At Upper Room Christian Cathedral, my current church in Manassas, Virginia, I've been blessed to find another pastor, Jesse Radford, III, who teaches and believes in doing what needs to be done based on tithes without the additional "assessments."

When my youngest son, Brien, started going down the wrong path, it was the Upper Room Christian Cathedral that turned him around. Brien joined a gang at age 13. He was suspended or expelled from every school he went to, including alternative ones. When he was 15 years old, he was sentenced to 13 months in jail for two charges involving physical violence. Minister Chris Parks mentored Brien while he was incarcerated, and by the time he was released, he was ready to make a change and began writing Christian rap. Since Ethan was absent from Brien's life and would have been a poor example if he had been present, men from the church, especially youth pastor Frank Lee, stepped in as mentors and role models. I am grateful to God for those men because they made such a positive difference in Brien's life.

No matter what I was going through in a marriage, at work, or with school, I had the most fun during family time with my children. It was total relaxation for me. I took them places every spring and summer. One vacation that stands out as a favorite was a trip to Charleston, South Carolina. Since Maurice was old enough to drive, he would meet us to be a part of these family trips. Whenever he had a job, he told them he was going to quit in the summer because his mother was going on vacation, and he was going, too. I couldn't believe that he would tell employers that! We still laugh about it today.

The family picture we took in Charleston was one of my favorites, but I don't have it anymore. It was confiscated by police years later when they busted down my door to arrest Brien. They seized it as "evidence" because they claimed the shirt he was wearing in the picture was proof of his gang ties. He was only four years old at the time the picture was taken. How ridiculous!

There was no conflict between Maurice and me on these family trips because Maurice wasn't under my authority. I couldn't parent him from afar, and I had decided that whatever transpired between him and Mama was what it was. When he was 18, I released myself of the worry, confusion, and pain, and stopped banging my head against the wall of their unified resistance to my intervention. Having Maurice with me had caused so much stress between Mama and me, so once he was in her care and I wasn't battling her for control over how to raise him, my relationship with her improved slightly.

As Maurice matured, his relationships with women concerned me. As far as I knew, they weren't violent, but they were volatile and never ended well. He had no respect for any woman who wasn't Mattie Lee McBride. I used to tell him, "Your grandmama is your girlfriend." He knew what I meant. There was no room in his heart for anyone else, and he was okay with that.

When my mother passed away, I was hurt, but I had tried to prepare myself for it. She was 95 years old and lived with me for most of the last six months of her life. By then, I had been living in Jacksonville, North Carolina, for about 11 years and was teaching Family and Consumer Science to high school students. Most of my career had been spent working with children and families. After working for the Department of Defense, I was a case manager for children with disabilities, and then a family and consumer science agent. I was always conflicted about my work in this field because the techniques that seemed to work for them didn't work with my oldest son. Each one of my four children are unique, and I had to use different strategies when raising each of them. I figured out what to do for everyone except Maurice. Nothing worked.

I cared for Mama as any loving daughter would. I fed her, cleaned her, and even baked chocolate chip cookies at night because, although she couldn't eat them, she loved the smell of them. One day, as I changed her diaper, she looked at me and said, "Lord, if anybody would have told me..." She didn't have to finish her statement.

"Well," I told her, "You did it for me when I was a little girl, so I'll do it for you." Luckily, these months we spent together helped heal our relationship before she died.

When Maurice had brought her to me from Waynesboro, she was eating and talking, but she stopped doing much of either within a few months. She would only drink nutritional shakes, and she would only talk if someone talked to her first. I had cared for Aunt Sammie Joe for the last couple of years of her life. Her son Charles was incarcerated, her husband had died, and she needed someone to look after her. She suffered from Alzheimer's disease, and her death had caught me by surprise, so when I saw these changes in Mama, I bought and read a book about dying. I could see her slipping away, and I tried to tell Maurice that she was dying, but he was in vehement denial about it.

I took Mama back to Maurice in Waynesboro when I planned a trip to Florida. I dropped my other children off, too, because they often spent summers there. It was the last time I saw her alive. I dropped her off, she got sick, and Maurice took her to the hospital. Since she wasn't eating, her doctor had given her a feeding tube, but for some reason, the feeding tube had been removed. A couple of days after my trip was over and I was back in North Carolina, I called the hospital. The nurse I spoke to couldn't explain why they were starving my mother. When I spoke to my mother, she said, "I just want to come home with you."

"I'm on my way," I told her. Regrettably, she died that afternoon before I could get there. I cannot describe the pain I felt; it can only be understood by those who have endured it. I managed to call my brother, and then I called Maurice. I wanted to tell him face-to-face, so I told him to meet me at the house and we would go to the hospital together, but he wouldn't agree to this unless I explained why, so I had to give him the news over the phone. He fell apart. I offered whatever comfort I could and arrived in Waynesboro that night. I tried my best to console him as I dealt with my own grief, but it was no use.

I know that the only reason my mama held on as long as she did was for Maurice. He was her reason for living, and she was his. When I had brought Maurice home from Boston two weeks after he was born, she had looked at him and said, "Lord, I wish I could see him grow up." God answered her simple prayer. The last 28 of her 95 years had been spent watching Maurice become a man. Still, he wasn't prepared to lose her. Mama's death hurt all of us, but Maurice was devastated. My brother Don and I were able to comfort each other, but because my relationship with Maurice was so damaged, he and I couldn't mourn together and instead, we dealt with the absence of my mama - *our* mama - without each other.

I often met Maurice's girlfriends and developed relationships with them, some closer than others. A few years after Mama died, one such relationship was with a girlfriend who came to live with me in Virginia at Maurice's request. I had moved there in 2004, the year following Mama's death, and was teaching child development in high school. This girlfriend needed a new start and Maurice was driving trucks, another effort to put some distance between him and his past. Although I had advised Maurice against

116

having a relationship with her because she was only separated, not divorced from her husband yet, I agreed that she could live with me and my two youngest children since Jon had moved out by then. We became close, so when her relationship with Maurice failed and he wanted me to put her out and cut off all communication, I wouldn't do it. This young woman was hundreds of miles away from her family and had nowhere else to go, and I was unwilling to evict her under such circumstances. Maurice was angry beyond words. After a huge blow up during which I had to call the police, he left my house and swore he wouldn't return as long as she was there.

The rift between us that had never really healed grew deeper. Even after the young woman moved out of my house, Maurice and I didn't see each other or talk to each other for at least six months. His absence hurt his sister, Avia, the most because they were very close. Frankly, it didn't bother me too much. I had warned him against being in a relationship with a married woman anyway. She was separated, but she was still married to her child's father and wasn't in a position to establish a serious relationship with another man. I had allowed her to stay with me against my better judgment, and their unhealthy relationship had ended just like I knew it would.

There had been a few girlfriends before the married one, and there was a relationship with a very young girl after that. I didn't think his relationships with any of them would last, so there was no need for me to develop relationships with every woman he dated. My second son had another child by another woman by then, so there was a bit of a revolving door there, too. All of these women entering my life and then leaving was too much for me! I don't think my sons ever understood the impact on my life, and my daughter's life. The women they were close to became like daughters to me and like sisters to Avia, so when their relationships with my sons ended, my daughter and I also felt the loss.

Consequently, when Maurice's relationship with Miss Young Thing ended, I told him not to introduce me to anyone else until *after* he was married. I didn't even want to come to the

117

wedding. He might have thought I was being mean, but I was just tired of having to "break up" with his girlfriends. Never being one to follow rules, he eventually introduced me to the next woman he established a relationship with. Luckily, she would be the last.

Chapter 10
A Great Loss

Maurice

When I was released from the detention center, I came home and saw that I had earned my GED. Mama had collected my mail the entire time I was locked up, and when I saw the results, I was excited! I was sure I had passed, but the confirmation set my mind at ease and prompted me to start thinking about my academic future. I was focused on being a rapper, of course, but as I said, I never wanted to be a dumb rapper, so this was important to me. Even though my mama and Vickie were unable to attend, I participated in the graduation exercise held in the Gilbert-Lambuth Memorial Chapel at Paine College. I didn't know then that God was giving me a peek into my future. Years later, I would return to that same chapel to address the freshman class of 2012, and eventually take my seat among the faculty during chapel every Wednesday morning as an Assistant Professor of Business.

My friend, Shawn, came to the ceremony to support me. Being locked up had changed my perspective on education enough that I was proud of earning my GED. My perspective changed again once I had money from my record deal, which came just a few months later. When I saw that $100,000 check, education faded to the background yet again. I understood that being educated meant greater earning potential, but it would be years before I understood the personal and social benefits of a college degree.

Generally speaking, I spent the first money I earned on an Acura Legend, studio equipment, and the house next door to Mama. When I was looking for a home to buy, she said, "You know the house next door is for sale." I knew what that meant.

"Okay, Mama" I said, and I bought it. I turned it into a studio that occasionally doubled as a bachelor pad. I usually kept a steady girlfriend, so I wasn't too wild, but there were times when my money and popularity created some interesting situations.

(That's all I'll say about that.) I was about business, so music was the primary focus when I was at that house. Most nights, I still slept in my mama's home. My current girlfriend was in college, and one day she suggested that I attend, too.

"For what?" I asked her. "I have money." She never brought it up again.

Having money meant I could do what I wanted to do. At the height of my career, I charged $15,000 to $20,000 per show, sharing the stage with artists like Do Or Die, Crucial Conflict, and OutKast. I spent quite a few dollars eating out, and I had a lot of fun with loads of friends. I didn't drink or smoke, so my money was spent on things like video games, clothes, shoes, jewelry, and tickets to theme parks. Six Flags in Atlanta, Georgia, was a favorite spot, and my friends and I made that drive often. I also went to Freaknik in Atlanta and Bike Week in Myrtle Beach. I was generous, but I managed my money well enough that I didn't have to work from ages 21 to 28 years old. I sat on a lot of money after reading financial information in jail. The worst financial mistake I made was not buying Bellsouth Mobility stock. I did the research, knew what move to make, and didn't make it. That would be the last time I would hesitate and lose.

I also indulged my mama as much as I could. She never asked for much, but when she did, I went overboard. If she asked for a doughnut, she got four dozen. If she asked me to rap for her friends, I stood right there in the living room and gave them a show. I was hot among the 70 to 90 demographic!

Before serving time, a DeVry University representative named Manny had visited me in my mama's home. I didn't revisit the option immediately after I got out, primarily because attending DeVry meant traveling to Atlanta, and the conditions of my probation prohibited that. When it became apparent that success in the music game didn't last forever, I knew I had to do something else to secure my future. Even while I was rapping, something kept telling me I needed a degree. That voice got louder as my record label dissolved, my money dwindled, and the number of shows I performed decreased. I had bought several cars by then, owning as many as five at a time. As I matured and my desire for the flashiness diminished, I sold a couple of them, gave away others, and kept a couple for my use.

As school became more of a priority, I considered options that would allow me to remain near home to care for Mama. She was almost 90 years old by now, and she needed me. She was on a fixed income, and although I was earning money, I wasn't earning enough to pay a nurse over $40 an hour for 24-hour care. Therefore, I became her primary caregiver.

I attended Augusta Technical College for about a year, but wasn't really required to learn. Girls carried my books to class for me, and my popularity earned my grades. Sometimes I traded concert tickets for passing scores. I knew this was wrong, but I thought it was all part of the game. I was being given something I hadn't earned, which is the way my entire life had been with mama. This was more of the same. In spite of this easy ride, when DeVry began offering accelerated online bachelor's degrees, I jumped at the opportunity. I didn't want to work for someone else, but I knew I would eventually need options, which meant I needed a degree.

I built my first computer when I built my studio, which was computer-based, in the house next door to Mama's. After my label dissolved, I was done with the music industry but still loved music, so I established my own record label, Nonstop Noize Entertainment, and continued to produce albums for Da Barnyard Click. I built my studio before I earned a degree from DeVry, so I did this based on my interest and talent, and by listening to the guys at the computer store who were happy to share what they knew.

While taking classes online, I worked on albums for other groups and was still connected to the industry. I rubbed elbows at Grammy parties and could still get Vickie access to some places and people she admired. I did shows with Lil' Jon, K.P. & Envyi, Soul for Real, Soundmaster T, and Ludacris. I had already met Ludacris, so when Lil' Jon introduced him as the rapper on the hit, "What's Your Fantasy," I wanted to kick myself. I had missed the opportunity to sign Ludacris to my label a few of years before. There were so many people always trying to get me to listen to

121

their demos that I didn't pay attention to him like I should have when he approached me. Later, on a visit to Ludacris' label, Def Jam South, I entered the lobby and was surrounded by pictures of him. I'm still not over that bad decision. It doesn't help that he's one of my wife Jessica's favorite rappers. When one of his songs comes on the radio, she smiles. I don't. When he makes an appearance on an awards show, she screams, "Luda!" I'm quiet. When the "Law & Order: SVU" episodes featuring Ludacris are on TV, she watches them every time. I scowl. "He's guilty," I tell her. "Ludacris killed two people!" She doesn't care. "Chris Lova Lova" can do no wrong.

Seriously though, I commend Ludacris and all of the other rappers who have successfully transitioned into other areas of entertainment, or who have become shrewd businessmen and businesswomen beyond the mic. It's a tough business, and longevity is still very rare, so I applaud those who are able to have long careers.

Since I was taking care of Mama, I had to say no to some of the better-paying shows in order to stay close to home. I couldn't be gone for days or weeks at a time like most other performers. Being responsible for her care was the same reason I had chosen DeVry's online degree. Mama had cared for me all of my life, and I had no qualms about doing the same for her. I had always called her Mama, and that's who she would always be to me. There was still a lot of tension between Vickie and me because of the undercurrent of unresolved issues. Thankfully, that didn't keep her from bailing me out of trouble when I needed it.

I could see that Mama was aging, but I was in denial about just how much her health was declining. After a few falls, she stopped walking and would spend all day in bed. Eventually the muscles in her legs began to contract, and she needed help relieving herself. She also experienced memory loss, stopped sleeping through the night, and was sometimes disoriented and unsure of the time of day. Yet, I couldn't fathom the thought of her absence. Her death was my greatest fear. When Vickie tried to tell me she was dying, I told her I didn't want to hear it. My mama was the only constant in my life and had always been a pillar of unconditional love and support. We were each other's reason for living.

Producing music, going to college, and caring for my mama required quite a juggling act. I didn't drop out of school because I don't believe in starting something I don't finish, and I didn't let music production go because it was my creative outlet and I loved it. There was no way I would let caring for my mama go; she was just too important. I struggled to keep all of the balls in the air. I was in the habit of doing what I had to do, so there was no time to whine about it. I had to sink or swim; no one was going to jump in and save me.

When Mama got really sick, I stopped touring all together and started producing other artists. I had nurses sitting with her during the day while I was in the studio next door. I fired one who wasn't treating her well. In retaliation, she filed a false report with the Division of Family and Children Services, unbeknownst to me, alleging that I was mistreating my mama. Anyone who knew me knew what a ridiculous lie that was. That false accusation led to other big problems, including a standoff with police when they tried to enter my home under the pretense of checking on her.

Although Vickie and Uncle Don lived miles away and weren't contributing financially to Mama's care, they always had a lot to say about it. They often tried to argue with me about her money, which they assumed I was mishandling, but that was ridiculous. I had my own money and would do anything in the world for Mama. I guess they based their assumptions on my past, but they were wrong. Yet, they vehemently defended me against DFCS. Go figure.

To protect Mama from DFCS, and to prevent myself from retaliating against the nurse who filed the false report against me, I took Mama to live with Vickie in Jacksonville, North Carolina. I didn't want to do it, but it was temporary; I didn't have another option, and I would NOT let DFCS take my mama from me. I was prepared to go to jail over it. I'm sure the standoff with police had shown them that.

Mama stayed with Vickie for about six months. I visited her while she was there, and I could see her declining. By this time, I had sold the hair salon to the partner I opened it with, I was still attending DeVry, and I was hosting a TV show, *On the Reel*, on UPN. I was also planning to open a nightclub in Macon, Georgia.

Vickie brought Mama back to Waynesboro on a Thursday, and dropped off Avia and Brien, too. I met them outside when they arrived and went to Mama immediately. I lifted her from the car and held her in my arms. "Mama, do you know who I am?" I asked.

She raised her head, looked at me, and smiled. "Maurice."

"Yeah. You're home now."

I carried her into my house where I had prepared a room for her. I chose my house because my brother and sister were recording a remake of "2D Frutti," and I could keep a closer eye on her at my house than next door at hers. By Monday, both Mama and my youngest brother Brien were sick. Mama was dehydrated, and Brien had a cold, so I took them both to the emergency room. The doctor gave Brien some medicine and sent him home, but decided to keep Mama. Once I sought medical help for her, DFCS learned that she was back in town and the harassment started again.

I visited Mama on Wednesday. When I walked into the room, she reached for me. I went to her bedside, embraced her, and kissed her. I sat with her for a while and shared a bag of Skittles before leaving to drop off my siblings in Warner Robins to visit their father, and then go to Macon. It was the last time I saw her alive. I talked to her on the phone on Thursday and Friday. On Friday night, my new nightclub earned $8,000. On Saturday, my mama was gone.

Vickie always says that Mama lived as long as she did because of me, and I lived for her. She was 95 years old when she died. I would have given everything to have her stay a while longer. I had prayed to God that she would live to be 100, but He had another plan.

Vickie came to Waynesboro and did her best to console me. She had given me the devastating news over the phone, and it had taken all I had to make it back there from Macon. She and Uncle Don handled most of the funeral arrangements.

I did the best I could to help, but I was in mourning and just barely able to function, so some details were overlooked. There was no obituary in the paper, for example, so the funeral was very small and very difficult.

I can't describe my sense of loss. My mama was gone. My advocate. My cheerleader. My supporter. *My mama.* Gone. Not only was I hurt, I was angry. Most of the people who attended the wake and funeral hadn't been to visit Mama in a very long time. She used to sit in the den and watch some of them walk by and say, "Look at them. They're walking right past my door and won't even stop to see how I'm doing." It bothered her then, and it was bothering me now. As I looked around the wake, I felt moved to speak for my mama.

I stood up. "I thank everybody for coming if you came to see her while she was alive. But the rest of y'all can leave. If you didn't come see her while she was alive, you don't need to be in here now." I meant that with everything in me. Their only response was sympathetic looks. Before I could continue, Vickie sat me down and tried to comfort me, but it was no use. Nothing could make this okay.

Eventually, Vickie addressed the people who were there to pay their respects. "I have to go back to North Carolina," she told them during her tearful remarks. "Please take care of my boy."

We buried my mama on a Friday. The funeral was the worst day of my life. I made it through, but I'll never be the same. I was a pallbearer, and carrying my mama into and out of Haven-Munnerlyn United Methodist Church was one of the hardest things I have ever had to do. After her casket was placed at the front, I took my seat next to Vickie on the front pew. When a funeral worker opened the casket for a final glance, I saw that a white cloth covered Mama's face and it made me hyperventilate. My mama couldn't breathe, and the thought took my breath away.

"Calm down," Vickie said. "She's not in there." She repeated this over and over, but I just couldn't breathe until a funeral worker removed the cloth from my mama's face. After the final viewing, I placed an autographed picture of me under her folded hands. It was the only way I could remain close to her.

I rode in the hearse to the gravesite. Everyone else rode in the family car. I had promised my mama that I would be with her all the way to the end, and I meant to keep that promise. There was a gaping hole in front of the tombstone that had been there for years. The first time I saw it, I was about ten years old, taking a shortcut through the cemetery to get to Pineland Bakery. Mama used to give me money to get a cream puff for me and doughnuts for her. When I saw the headstone with her name on it, I started crying and ran back home.

"What's wrong?" she asked when I came back in the house.

"I just saw a gravestone with your name on it!" I wept.

"Well you see me sitting right here, don't you?" she said matter-of-factly.

"Yeah..."

"Well, alright then," she said. And just like that, I was okay. I dried my tears and went back through the cemetery to the bakery.

The graveside service is a blur. I think it was the standard "ashes to ashes, dust to dust" kind of thing. I do remember taking two pink roses from a wreath and tossing one onto her casket as it was lowered into the ground. I kept the other one, which I still have today.

My mind knew my mama was gone, but my heart couldn't process the loss. I'm sure Vickie, Uncle Don, and other relatives were grieving, too, but no one could help me deal with my bereavement. I started spending time in the cemetery across the street from our house, sitting at her gravesite in a chair I dragged there. One night as I sat at her grave, a police officer showed up.

"Sir, what are you doing out here?" he asked. I didn't answer. He repeated the question, and when I didn't reply, he called for backup. I don't know what he thought I was doing, and I didn't care. I didn't know where else to go or what else to do. I didn't care if they took me to jail. My mama was gone. My defender. My best friend. My lifeline. *My mama.* Gone.

I wept openly. The first officer who responded to the call approached us calmly. She recognized me as I sat there staring at

126

the newly occupied grave that I had been talking to for hours, and that had been marked for decades. "Maurice?"

"Yes, ma'am?"

"Are you okay?" she asked.

"Yes ma'am."

She looked at the other officer. "Leave him alone," she told him. He didn't ask any questions, and they left me there.

While the void my mama's death left in my life was still fresh, Uncle Don died just a few months later on Thanksgiving day. He had been battling drug addiction for years and had died of an overdose. He died while visiting Augusta, so I had to identify the body, and tell my mother and his only son that he was gone. I participated in his homegoing service in a haze.

My goal became to keep as many things in place in my life as possible that were present when my mama was alive. Angel had been my last girlfriend, so I tried to hold on to her for that reason. It wasn't a good decision, and I eventually decided to move on. Holding on to relationships or anything else wasn't going to bring my mama back. With the help of a couple of friends and my cousin, Don Jr., who became more like a brother after his father died, I began to spend more time among the living.

I moved back into the house where I was raised and rented out the home I owned next door, but I needed more income. Although I'd missed some big opportunities, I had handled my money well enough to live almost eight years without working. Now, I needed a job. Sitel, a company that operates a local call center, was hiring, so I applied and began my short career in customer service. I was at an all-time low. My mama was dead, and I had gone from being M.C. Moo, commanding up to $20,000 a show, to being an Internet CSR, earning $8 an hour. I had made other attempts to earn money the "normal" way, like telemarketing and selling Kirby vacuum cleaners door to door as I transitioned out of the music industry, but they were all short-lived. Needless to say, I didn't enjoy working at Sitel. It was an orphanage for the unemployed; a place to work until we could find real jobs. People were always shocked when they found out I was working at Sitel.

Their question was always the same. "What happened?" they would ask incredulously.

"Life," I told them. My response wasn't much of an answer, but it was all I could say. It was much easier than trying to explain that part of me had died and was buried across the street from where I slept every night, and that I was just trying to hold on. They wouldn't understand that the loss of my muse had killed the most creative part of me, and it was all I could do to not go to the graveyard with a shovel, or ingest enough medicine to take me to my resting place alongside her.

It was an incredibly dark time in my life. I cried, slept, ate, worked, and cried some more. I felt guilty for the times my misbehavior and bad decisions had made my mama cry, and for shedding so many tears now that she wasn't here anymore because she had always said, "Baby, don't cry for me when I'm gone. I've lived a long life." I tried to remember her words and focus on the time I'd been blessed to have her in my life, but the weeping endured. I prayed and prayed and prayed, begging God for His mercy to see me through this painful time. I was alive and breathing, but I wasn't living. It was only my faith in God that kept me from taking drastic action to end the pain, and that slowly helped me realize that my life was still worth living even though the person I had lived for was gone.

I worked at Sitel for six months before I quit and moved to Jacksonville, North Carolina, where Vickie and my siblings had been living for a few years. I took my current girlfriend with me. Vickie had taken the loss of her brother hard, and I knew she needed all of her children together. She had prepared herself for the loss of Mama, but Uncle Don's death was sudden. Their relationship had been close, and his death shook her to the core. Additionally, she owned a daycare center, and I helped her operate it. I was still trying to finish school, and I thought her support would help. We needed each other; yet, we still didn't get along. I didn't have to pay any bills, but Vickie's overbearing intrusion into my personal life was unbearable. The physical altercations between us had ended long ago, but we were fundamentally very different people, and the loss of two loved ones hadn't changed that.

I lived in Jacksonville for just a few months, through the summer of 2004, and when Vickie got a job in Virginia, I moved back to Waynesboro. My girlfriend had moved back to Georgia before that. A couple of months in the house with Vickie had brought that relationship to a swift end. It wasn't wise to foster a relationship between my girlfriends and Vickie. She always advocated for them, no matter what, and I was always the one who was wrong.

Before Mama's death, girls could come and go; it really wasn't that serious. I had my mama and I had my music. That was all I needed. Her love was unconditional and unmatchable. After Mama's death, however, I felt like I had to develop a strong bond with someone, so I started dating to marry. Sometimes that caused me to hold on too long to relationships that probably never should have existed. My most damaging relationship cost me my SUV, my house, and too much of my money, so Mama's home, which she had willed to me, remained my primary residence. She knew that I had been forced to spend some nights on the streets when I lived with Vickie. When Mama explained that the house would be mine, she said, "Baby, no one will ever be able to put you out. This house is yours, and everything in it."

I also tried harder to re-establish the bond Vickie and I had shared in my early years, although I had been unsuccessful in doing so prior to losing Mama. The Christmas before Mama died, we traveled to Jacksonville to spend the holiday with Vickie, Uncle Don, and my siblings. At some point during that visit, I pulled Vickie to the side and said, "Look, I want us to have a better relationship." She shot me down immediately.

"It's too late for that," she told me. "Matt Lee ruined any chance of that," she said definitively, and walked away. I didn't approach her about it anymore until after Mama died.

I was still living in my inherited home years later when I met Dr. Jessica Wallace, the woman I would marry, who is also the author of this book. She is a quality woman who reminds me of my mama - a sophisticated, classy, educator who believed in doing the right thing. Mama was financially responsible, and was very much a disciplinarian who believed in children being children. And she never told me what I couldn't do. No matter what happened in her life, Mama remained who she was. On the day my uncle died, Vickie and I learned that he was my grandfather's "outside child," the result of an affair with a woman who lived in the projects. I can only imagine the hell my grandfather caught behind that decision, but my mama loved and raised my Uncle Don as her own. My wife is an educator who is fiscally responsible and loves children in a similar way. I know she wouldn't deal with an outside child, though, and I wouldn't expect her to. Times have changed, and I'm not crazy.

I still feel the loss of my mama, but the unconditional love, support, and understanding I get from my wife help me cope. Jessica helps me understand myself and my behaviors, which helps me make better decisions. Having her in my life also helped me forgive my mother and my father. Jessica is a natural counselor, and many things she has said to me over the years have helped me heal the little boy inside me who was hurt and never got the chance to understand why. I've made peace with him, and my on-going healing led to me being able to forgive both of my parents. Once I accepted that I couldn't go back, I made the decision to go forward and not try to live in the past.

I still called my mother "Vickie" up to and following Mama's death. That changed when the girlfriend I took to North Carolina with me told me it hurt her feelings. I had never known that. Despite our volatile history, I never wanted to hurt my mother, so I haven't called her Vickie since. She is Mother Dear. My mama is gone, but my mother is still here.

Another reason I returned to Waynesboro when my mother moved to Virginia was so that I could continue to qualify for the Georgia Equalization Grant. I graduated from DeVry University with a bachelor's degree in Business Administration a year and a half after Mama died. My mother was finally proud of something I had done. She had pushed me to stay the course after we lost Mama, had helped me financially when she could, and had occasionally sent me care packages. Commencement was held at the Atlanta Civic Center. My mother and siblings came, and I tried to put on a happy face, but it was a struggle because I was so sad that Mama wasn't there. I wished with all of my heart that she could have seen me earn that degree. I missed her with everything in me.

At this point in my life, survival was primary, and music was secondary. My mama had been my inspiration, and a part of my creativity went with her to the grave. While in North Carolina, I had decided to go to law school to "fight the power." I wanted to advocate for those who were being held back because of past mistakes. I changed, and I believe other people can, too, but it seems as though no one wants to give a chance to anyone whose background isn't perfectly clean. While preparing for the LSAT and exploring my options, I still had to live, so I became a licensed industrial electrician while applying for jobs in my degree field, most of which were in Atlanta. Since my new girlfriend, Sarah, had family in Savannah, Georgia, I accepted a job as an electrician on the night shift for about a month and a half, running bologna cable, installing transformers, and running cable trays six days a week, for 12 hours a day, and earned $15 per hour, plus overtime. The money was good at the time, but the work was dangerous and exhausting.

I decided to go to graduate school since my GPA was not high enough for law school. My struggle to work, produce music, and take care of Mama, and then deal with her death, made earning high grades difficult, and there was a question as to whether or not I would be allowed to take the bar exam because of my criminal history. I determined that a better course of action would be to get my master's degree first, then apply to law school.

American InterContinental University advertised a 10-month MBA program, and every student who was accepted into the program and enrolled in classes would be given a laptop. I applied, was accepted, and enrolled. I had classes every Thursday night in Atlanta, which was a three-hour drive away. I made the weekly trip with two friends who were working on their bachelor's degrees.

I decided to open a WIC (Women, Infants, and Children) store with my girlfriend, Sarah. That didn't work out well, and I eventually had to close it. In fact, the relationship didn't work out well, and I eventually had to end it. Since I had lived with some of her relatives while working in Savannah, when she needed a fresh start, I sent her to Virginia to live with Vickie. That's when she started seeing another man while living in my mother's house. I was never sure of Vickie's role in all of that, and her refusal to evict Sarah immediately drove us further apart. Vickie and I didn't talk for months, and we didn't see each other for longer than that.

In hindsight, I should have let Sarah go way before then, but I was so wrapped up in the love I felt from her family that I held on to her long after I realized it wouldn't work. When the relationship ended, I felt the loss of everyone.

After seeing an 18-wheeler roll by my WIC store one day before it closed, I decided to get a commercial driver's license, drive for a trucking company during the week, and switch to AIU's Saturday program. I sold the store and started contacting truck-driving schools. The one I attended in Paducah, Kentucky, is where I experienced a negative reaction to being college educated for the first time. It was total culture shock. I was told I would never be a truck driver, so I decided to be the best in the class. I was eventually cut from the program because of my background check. That decision left me broke and stranded in Paducah. An ex-girlfriend sent me a bus ticket to get back home.

In order to attend truck driving school, I had missed two weeks of classes at AIU, but had submitted homework assignments online, so I was doing okay. I tried another truck driving school in Florida. I met all the criteria for Cypress Trucking, and they also guaranteed I would be home on the weekends for school. I earned my CDL in three weeks, but couldn't work for them because of traffic tickets on my driving record. I soon found a company willing to hire me, but it was in Tulsa, Oklahoma. Since I had missed four of the five required class meetings at AIU, I had to drop out of the class, which left me owing a $6,000 balance. Luckily, I was able to transfer the one class I had completed to AIU Online, which was a separate entity, and become an online

132

graduate student while driving trucks. This was perfect since I couldn't come home weekly and was often over the road for two or three weeks at a time.

I earned my master's degree all over the country, stopping at free Wi-Fi spots to post to discussions, submit assignments, and do research. Being a truck driver allowed me to visit 46 of the contiguous 48 states, missing only North and South Dakota. The United States is truly a beautiful country, and driving trucks allowed me to see places and things I would never have seen otherwise. Driving trucks also gave me plenty of time to think about my life and my childhood. Sometimes the memories were upsetting, but sometimes I laughed out loud at the way I used to think. As a small boy, I thought Georgia was the whole country. Everywhere I went at that time was in Georgia – Waynesboro, Augusta, Statesboro, Savannah. I also thought Jesus was the king of Georgia because when I went to church – which I did every Sunday whether I rode with neighbors or walked since my mama often couldn't make it – we sang the song, "Soon and very soon, we are going to see the King..." Well, I didn't want to miss that! So, even though I ignored some other things Mama told me to do, I went to church every Sunday because I wanted to be there when we went to see Jesus Christ, the King of Georgia.

During a snowstorm on I-35 in Amarillo, Texas, traffic came to a standstill. I had a five-page essay due in three hours and less than a quarter of a tank of diesel in the eighteen wheeler. I had to choose between running the truck so that I could complete my paper and risk running out of fuel, or turning it off to conserve fuel and be ready to go when traffic moved so I could deliver the load I was carrying. I chose to let the truck run so that I could complete my paper and, luckily, didn't run out of diesel. I enjoyed traveling the country, but knew I wanted more stability, and knew I wouldn't be a truck driver forever.

A friend of mine liked to joke that I was the world's worst truck driver, but I was doing what I had to do. Being committed to doing well in school meant that I was sometimes late with deliveries, which meant I didn't get the most loads or the best-paying loads. Still, I survived. I ate enough, although I didn't eat

133

well. I had no wife, no children, no mortgage, minimal debt, and low bills. Being a truck-driving graduate student was working for me.

Eventually, I decided to buy my own truck, which meant I had to earn more to make payments. Shortly after, I let the truck go back to the company because it required that school be placed on the back burner. I had dropped out of school for about six months in order to earn more money to make the high weekly payments, but returned after the truck payments stopped.

My relationship with Vickie was still strained. After the incident with Sarah, I had to stay away to avoid hating her. She was happy that I was in the MBA program, but sometimes it seemed like she wanted me to quit. I don't know why. It may have been because, depending on the time of year and the type of truck, the work can be really dangerous. She had also nursed me back to health when I caught pneumonia. She may have thought I was trying to do too much.

I continued to drive trucks, but I was always looking for a job related to my academic training that would allow me to start building a career. I was hired as a substitute teacher at the alternative school in my hometown with the goal of teaching full time. Before the full time job began, I was helping some students with their music goals. They formed a rap group, and since I was still well-known for my producing capabilities, people often sought my help. An argument with one of the group members turned violent when he refused to leave my home and threatened to kill me. We fought, and that incident invalidated the school board's job offer.

While completing my master's degree, I was offered a job at Virginia College's Augusta campus as an adjunct professor. It didn't pay much, but I had very few bills, so it was okay. I appreciated the experience. I was also working a little for Candy Coated Entertainment, whose biggest client, Katt Williams, was starting his own music label and introducing a new artist, Klutch. I went back to driving trucks after I lost the job at Virginia College, most likely because of the background check. I earned my master's degree about a month later.

Once again, I found myself in the Atlanta Civic Center preparing to march to "Pomp and Circumstance." There had been some issues when I applied for graduation. Driving trucks and trying to survive had taken its toll; I had earned two C's and the graduate program allowed a maximum of one. I challenged the policy by filing an appeal, and as they reviewed my petition, the $6,000 debt I owed at the Atlanta campus surfaced. The only way I could move forward was by adding another concentration to my degree program, which I did. It required taking more classes, but I graduated with an MBA with a double concentration in marketing and management in 2008. Unsurprisingly, I got fired from a trucking job for late deliveries around the same time.

I wasn't expecting Vickie to attend the commencement ceremony because she told me she had to work. My friend William (DJ Big Bang) drove me to Atlanta, and I hoped that he, along with some of my friends who lived in or near the city, would be my cheering section. I understood that Vickie had to work, so I was disappointed but not upset. Besides, she paid for my cap and gown, and I really appreciated that.

I knew my father, Phillip, wouldn't be there. In January 2007, I'd taken him to breakfast. I had decided to try to establish a relationship with him, but I knew that couldn't happen without my questions being answered. He owed me that. Plus, I was paying for the meal. It was now or never.

"Where were you?" I asked him after our food was served. "When my brother's dad came to get him, I didn't have anybody. When my friends' dads took them fishing, I didn't have anybody. Even when I was invited along sometimes, I still didn't have a dad." There were tears in my eyes. He listened quietly as I told him about the pain his absence had caused. I didn't care that I was the result of a non-consensual act. I was here and hadn't asked to be, so I deserved an explanation. "You have no idea what I've been through," I told him. "I could have avoided a lot of the pain I experienced if I had a father. I needed a father," I cried.

Phillip stared at me, and then hung his head. After a few minutes of silence, he explained that he was young and had gone to the military before I was born. Obviously there were other reasons he felt he couldn't be active in my life, but those remained unspoken. After his explanation of sorts, he said, "Well, I can't change any of that, but from this point on, I promise I'll try to do better." I felt hopeful, and since then, he really has tried to be a part of my life. It's not easy for either of us.

Some people have asked how I could have a relationship with Phillip knowing what he did to my mother. Actually, my mother is one of the reasons I am able to have a relationship with him. She has somehow found it in her heart to not make me feel guilty about my need for my father in my life, and I love her for that. I don't think most people could do it. Another reason I can forgive my father is that I've done so much for which I need forgiveness, it would be hypocritical for me to withhold it from anyone else.

Whether there was one person there or one hundred, I still planned to cross the stage in Atlanta. To my delight, everyone I gave a ticket to showed up, and my mother and godmother surprised me, too. My godmother, Tanya Swearingen, lived in Atlanta, and my mother had flown in and was in the civic center when the graduates entered. I heard her unmistakable voice call my name and looked around to find her in the audience. "You know I wasn't going to let my child graduate and I not be here," she told me later. That , along with her help over the past few months, neutralized my feelings about the role she had played in my most recent break-up. It felt great to have her there. To show my appreciation of the effort she put into supporting me, I gave her my satin stole as a keepsake. She flew back home the same day with a picture of us in hand, and I went to celebrate my accomplishment with my friends.

My mother and I had school in common, but for different reasons. She pursued degrees to increase her earning potential; I pursued them to fight injustice. I had proven to myself that all of the naysayers were wrong, and I wanted to help other people prove this to their naysayers as well. When my mother had earned her master's degree, I was still heavily involved in the music scene. Now I had mine, and my dream had changed. I still loved music, but it wasn't my primary focus. There are many songs that I love that got me through tough times or inspired me, like Kirk Franklin's "Imagine Me," but at this point, music didn't consume me as it once had. I had more learning to do. This MBA had brought me one step closer to a law degree, and it also qualified me to teach. Teaching wasn't my calling, but I wanted to make a difference. I would do what I had to do until I could do what I wanted to do.

Chapter 11
Two Paths Converge

Vickie

At the same time that Maurice began the MBA program at American InterContinental University, I started a doctoral program at Walden University. When I began my college career as the 17-year-old single parent of a preschooler, earning a doctorate was not my goal. My mother had earned a bachelor's degree, and I knew I needed one. I earned the master's degree because an opportunity presented itself, and I took advantage of it. I chose to pursue the doctorate because, after three failed marriages, it had become clear to me that I was going to be a single parent, so I had to position myself so that I could always take care of my children. Not only did I want to meet their basic needs, I also wanted to give them a variety of experiences that would make them well-rounded people. The more education I had, the better my chances were of providing my family with what they needed.

When Maurice finished his master's degree, I was still working on my doctorate at Walden. To say that I wasn't enjoying the experience is an understatement. I hated it, and I felt like giving up, but I had never backed down from a challenge before, and I wasn't about to start now. Still, I was miserable and receptive to other terminal degree opportunities.

In 2008, I was in Dallas, Texas, at a work-related conference. I saw a booth set up for Capella University. Maurice had mentioned this school to me and was planning to earn his doctorate from there. He knew how much I hated my current program and had encouraged me to consider Capella. Well, here I was at the intersection of time and opportunity. I visited their booth and talked to a representative about where I was in my current program. I was reluctant to switch schools because I didn't want to lose any of the credits I had earned already. I liked what I heard and decided to apply. I called Maurice and told him my decision. He had been in communication with the university before now, so he continued his application process. Luckily for both of us, they accepted our graduate work and applied it to our doctoral programs. In January 2009, we both started our first classes at Capella University.

As I worked on my doctorate, I didn't have a social life. When I realized how strenuous earning this degree was going to be, I eliminated almost any and every thing that was not directly related to my success in the doctoral program. On the rare occasion that I wanted to go somewhere on the weekend, I completed all of my assignments mid-week so I could be worry-free and enjoy myself. After I completed the coursework and entered the dissertation phase, I tried establishing one romantic relationship, but it was unsuccessful. He didn't seem to understand my role as the single parent of adult children, and I have no room in my life for anyone whose presence limits what I can do for my family. Furthermore, it soon became clear that he wasn't looking for a serious commitment, and I am far past casual dating. So, as it got tougher and tougher to juggle my job as a middle school family and consumer science teacher, parent young adults, be a student, and develop a relationship, something had to go. I chose to end the relationship, and I do not regret the decision.

Major life events happened during the doctoral degree program, including the high school graduation of my two youngest children and the births of three more grandchildren, one from Jon and two from Avia. After graduation, Avia and Brien both remained at home and began their transitions into adulthood. Of course, I always encouraged my children to earn college degrees, and once Maurice realized how this investment in yourself could pay off, he reinforced my message by offering his own support and encouragement to his siblings over the years.

My daughter Avia got pregnant almost immediately after she graduated from high school. I was devastated by her decision to become a parent instead of a college graduate. I repeated the conversations my mother had had with me and offered the same support I had been given when she gave birth to a daughter. Even as a full time doctoral student with a full time job, I took on the role of primary caregiver to allow Avia to focus on school from

139

Sunday through Thursday. I fed the baby, changed her, and got up with her during the night. From Friday to Sunday, my daughter was responsible for doing these things.

However, my message about doing what I did in order to have what I had didn't impact her the same way, so being successful in school wasn't her primary goal. It wasn't a "do or die" situation like it was for me. It soon became clear that my daughter had no interest in school. She failed every class her first year and decided to work instead. She is a hard worker and has never complained about having a job, so I'm happy about that. Before her daughter was two, Avia became pregnant again. Needless to say, I wasn't happy, and although I had taken on the primary responsibility for her first child, I refused to do the same for her son, my first grandson. She had failed to see the impact her decisions had on her life and mine, and if I continued to be "super grandma," she would never understand. Regardless, I still hope and pray that she will realize the value of a good education and do what she has to do to secure a future for herself and her children.

Brien, on the other hand, changed the course of his life after being incarcerated. He earned an advance diploma and graduated from high school with honors. He will graduate with an associate's degree from Nova Community College soon, and plans to earn a bachelor's degree. He is also an amazingly talented Christian rapper who goes by the moniker T.A.G. (This Anointed Generation). Although they have different fathers and were born 17 years apart, my oldest son and youngest son are so much alike, it's uncanny. Just like Maurice, Brien loves music, spent time incarcerated as a teenager, and was able to turn his life around when he realized and accepted the presence of God in his life. Brien is definitely the man of God I was told he would be and strives every day to be more Christ-like. He is intelligent, compassionate, and honest, and is eager to share the word of God and the love of Jesus Christ with everyone. I couldn't be more proud of my baby boy.

As the stress of my frenzied juggling act mounted, there were many times when I wanted to quit. Sometimes I questioned whether or not this was all really worth it. After all, I had a master's degree and years of experience in my field, and all of my children were grown. But there was something in me that wouldn't let me give up, and I knew Maurice didn't want to do this without me. Besides, I had started working towards a goal, and I was still setting an example for my children and modeling the kind of behavior I wanted to see in them. Instead of giving up, I did what I had to do instead of what I wanted to do. I simply wasn't a quitter, and when Maurice wanted to give up, I reminded him that he wasn't a quitter, either. There were instances when we both talked each other down from the ledge, and it worked. We didn't give up, and we persevered, but it took will. We stumbled and we faltered, but we didn't fall.

Although I was very clear about my lack of desire to meet any other woman before he married her, Maurice is who he is, so I met Dr. Jessica Wallace. She was presented to me as an expert scholar of sorts, and it was months before I knew they were in a relationship. I had no reason to believe that this relationship would be any different than the others, but he held on to her. As I got to know her, I realized that if there was anyone who could handle the madness that is my son, it was her. He has met his match, and I thank God for her.

Jessica proved to be an invaluable resource to both Maurice and me during the comprehensive exam and dissertation phase of our doctoral programs. I chose to write my dissertation about the impact of the child development associate credentialing process on child care provider performance, so Jessica's background in education was helpful. As our journey beyond the doctorate progresses, she continues to offer great support, an example of which is her willingness to help us tell our story by writing this book. Maurice has told me that Jessica reminds him of Mama, and I agree.

I didn't view going to school with Maurice as unusual. With so many older adults returning to school these days, I heard of parents and children going to school together all of the time. It didn't really hit me that we had done something wonderful and unique until it was done. *I* am a doctor. *My son* is a doctor. We did this together. *Wow.*

141

Maurice

After earning my MBA, I was still focused on preparing for the LSAT. *Should I take the chance?* I wondered. It was possible that I could invest the time and money into a law degree and then not be allowed to sit for the bar. I sincerely wanted to fight the good fight and advocate for those without a voice, but I didn't know if I'd be allowed to do that because of my past. An academic counselor told me there were things I could do, like community service, to counteract my previous mistakes, so I volunteered at the local nursing home. It was one of the best decisions I ever made. I have so much respect and love for the elderly, and I feel honored when they share what they know with me.

During a trip to Orlando, Florida, I hung out with a friend who was a practicing lawyer and a professor at Florida A&M University's College of Law. Our conversation about my quandary went something like this:

Lawyer: "What kind of law do you want to practice?"

Me: "Criminal law."

Lawyer: "How are you going to get paid? The people you'll most likely be defending can't afford a lawyer."

Me: "Okay, I'll do corporate law."

Lawyer: "How many of them do you think look like you? If there's a black person at the table, it will most likely be a woman - a double minority."

Me: Blank stare. He quickly reloaded his weapon to shoot more holes through my dreams.

"A good private practice will take at least ten years to build," the attorney said. By the time you finish law school and build your practice, you'll be how old?" He asked a lot of good questions, but didn't seem to have any good answers. I told him so. He smiled.

"Look, man. Why do you want to be part of the cure when you could be a part of the prevention?" he asked. "If you want to advocate for people, earn a doctorate. You can fight with a doctorate. You can only defend with a law degree." I didn't know how I could fight with a doctorate, but I trusted his opinion, so I started exploring doctoral programs.

Since I had gotten another job driving trucks to make a living, I knew that I couldn't do a traditional doctoral program, so I researched non-traditional ones. By this time, my mother had already started a doctoral program, but I knew she hated it. A friend of mine was attending the same school and felt the same way, so that wasn't an option for me. As I did more research and talked to more people, Capella University emerged as a frontrunner. They would accept some of my MBA credits towards a Ph.D., and another friend of mine had earned his doctorate from Capella in two years. He had nothing but great things to say about his experience at Capella.

When I told my mother about my decision to earn a Ph.D. instead of a J.D., she was neutral about it, neither encouraging nor discouraging. It may have been because she was having such a difficult time in her doctoral program. A part of me still felt like my mistakes still caused her to doubt my vision at times, but I couldn't be sure. Since I knew she hated her current school, I suggested that she attend Capella University with me. No matter how old we get, we are still children in our parents' eyes, so she didn't immediately take my advice. I didn't give up, though, and continued to encourage her to switch schools. As God would have it, she attended a conference in Texas where she talked to a representative from Capella. When she called me to tell me she was thinking about transferring, I told her about my friend who earned his degree in two years and enjoyed the program. She made the decision to transfer, and I moved forward with my application. In January 2009, we began the arduous journey to earn our terminal degrees together.

Driving trucks while going to school didn't get any easier. Sometimes I still had to choose between delivering a load on time and submitting an assignment on time. I usually chose to submit the assignment and be late with the load. Driving trucks was a way to make a living while I earned my doctorate; it wasn't going to be a career for me. However, I came to understand how the

143

transportation industry could be lucrative. Somehow, the most important people in the equation, the drivers, were the lowest paid and most disrespected. The only way drivers can earn the kind of money they deserve is by owning their own trucks, so in 2010, shortly before completing my doctoral comprehensive examination, I purchased a truck from a driver I met in Tulsa, Oklahoma. We agreed upon a payment plan, and I made my final payment in 2013.

I continued to work in the trucking industry throughout my doctoral program, and I branched out into other areas. In addition to working as an adjunct and full time associate professor of business at several schools, Jessica and I co-authored a children's book, *Oliver Vance, Pull Up Your Pants!* in 2011. My talented friend Groove, the same one who produced the track for 2D Frutti, illustrated it. I wanted to write a story to address the sagging pants issue and teach boys and young men that perception is reality, and that they need to take responsibility for and control of the message they send when they dress a certain way.

I'd enjoyed writing stories since I was a child, and I had written many rap songs by then, but writing a book was a little different. The idea had come to me a year or two before, but it didn't become a reality until I met Jessica. With her writing skills and extensive background in education, she was able to develop my draft into something amazing. We also created The Oliver Vance Project, which is based on the book. The project includes a character education program that teaches children and young adults to have the courage to be themselves, and focuses on goal setting, decision-making, and positive individuality. So while I was writing my dissertation, we were selling books and doing Oliver Vance presentations throughout the southeast. This was just one of the many ways Jessica changed my life, so I decided to change her last name. We got married shortly after graduation.

I chose to write my dissertation about human resource managers' attitudes toward hiring non-violent ex-offenders who had earned degrees. It was unchartered territory; the research in this area was very limited. This meant that my dissertation committee members were learning about this topic along with me.

A classmate tried to convince me to change my topic, telling me that no one cared about ex-offenders. Well, I cared, because I had lived the research. I'd had job offers rescinded after employers ran background checks, so it was obvious that a criminal record could haunt me continuously, no matter how old the convictions were, and no matter what degrees I earned. I empathized greatly with the struggle of the ex-offender, so I stuck with my topic and it paid off.

The coursework had been challenging, but the dissertation was extremely difficult. Everything was so subjective and there was no sure way to tell if I was on the right track or not. The process was frustrating and disheartening because I wasn't sure I was making progress, and my student loan debt continued to increase. There were so many times that I wanted to quit, and I said as much to Jessica many times. I had an MBA, and experience in my field. Besides, I was a published author. I could do a ton of things without a Ph.D.! Since she had earned her doctorate from Florida A&M University before we met, she assured me that everyone went through this tedious process; schools weren't just handing out doctorates. Because my mother and I were on this journey together, she wouldn't let me quit, either. "We are not quitters," Vickie told me repeatedly. A few weeks later, I would have to repeat these same words to her when she was dealing with a setback or was faced with another unexpected hurdle.

Despite the difficulty, I knew it had to be done. I'm not in the habit of starting things that I don't finish, and I needed this degree to take me further into my future and put more miles between me and my past. Education was the great equalizer. I had to reach this goal no matter what. Well, not only did I reach it, I did it with my mother by my side. For most of my life, I felt as though she never understood what I was going through when I faced difficult situations. Earning a doctorate was the one struggle in my life that I was sure she understood because, although I majored in Organization and Management and she majored in K-12 Studies in Education, she experienced it with me. Instead of arguing and fighting against each other, we fought together toward a common goal. Instead of causing each other pain, we helped each other through painful times. For once, we were on the same side.

As we neared the end of our doctoral degree programs, I knew that what we were about to accomplish was unique. No one had ever heard of a mother and child earning doctorates from the same school at the same time, and each time I shared what we were doing, people were amazed. When it was all said and done, our story went viral on the Internet, and we were later featured in the February 2014 edition of *Ebony* magazine. My mother and I did something great, and we did it together. What more could a son ask for?

Chapter 12
Dynamic Duo

Vickie

From my seat among the graduates at the Minneapolis Convention Center in Minneapolis, Minnesota, I listen as Mr. Kinney reads a story about Maurice and me. I didn't realize he was talking about us until he said, "Now here's the mother's response."

Nobody but God, I think as I listen to the university president's brief re-cap of my life. I am excited and emotional; overcome by a spirit of thankfulness for God's grace. My life could have been ruined so many times. There are some things I wish I had never experienced, and there are decisions I wish I hadn't made, but I thanked God for His endless love, patience, and forgiveness. Because of His unconditional love and mercy, I was with my first born son, doing what no other mother and child had done before. No one could have known, but God knew. He knew when I was born to a young mother in YDC, and adopted by a God-fearing woman, that something great was in my future. He knew when I was forced to have sex and became pregnant at just 13 years old that there would be incredible glory in my story. He knew when I gave birth to a son at 14 and chose to keep him, love him, raise him, and fight the streets for him that our tumultuous relationship would be healed, and we would help each other reach our goals.

Maurice had been my motivation when I began my voyage into higher education 30 years earlier, and he was my support as I reached the end of it with my terminal degree. I was angry with him for so long, but I have forgiven him for all the pain he caused me, and I hope he has found it in his heart to do the same for me. If it had not been for the opportunity to share this moment with Maurice, it's unlikely that I would have even attended commencement. I had crossed the stage two or three times before, so that part wasn't the big deal. Being here with my son was.

147

This commencement exercise put the shine on my academic and personal life. Mama always said to reach for the moon, and if you don't make it, grab a star on the way down. When I visited Waynesboro after graduation, I walked through the cemetery across the street from our house and went to my mother's grave. I didn't go there often because she had given us specific instructions about visiting her burial place. "Don't come out there bothering me," she always told us. "Let me sleep!" I smiled as I remembered her words, placed the medallion I had been given at graduation around the plant holder at the base of her headstone, and thought, *Well, Mama, I made it to the moon, and I grabbed a few stars on the way up!*

I have finally achieved enough to help me provide for my children. Although they are all adults now, I am still responsible for guiding them into their destiny, and making sure they have the tools and skills to live good, secure lives. Initially, I wanted to make sure they didn't grow up having less than I had, and that was no small feat. Now, I wanted them to have more than I had, and have the tools to maintain a certain level of living as independent adults.

As long as I live, I will strive to set a good example for them and my seven grandchildren (so far). Since my mother and brother are gone, it is up to me to establish a legacy for my family. Other than the fact that I was born to a teenage mother in YDC, I don't know much about my birth parents, so I have tried to break the curse of negativism and establish a new, positive tone for my children. I haven't actively pursued finding out about my birth parents, in part because I don't want to run the risk of bringing something or someone into my children's or grandchildren's lives that might contradict what I have established. My own poor decisions have provided more than enough non-examples. I plan to be a little more aggressive about it, however, since I promised my children I'd find out what I could about my family's medical history.

When people hear my story, they often focus on me being a teenage mother who defied stereotypes, and if that is useful to someone, so be it. Some may use it to support their position as pro-lifers or to advocate for adoption. That's fine, too. The message I would like to promote, however, isn't about that. It's about determination and persistence. It is about defining yourself on your own terms, and not allowing your circumstances to define you. I was determined and persistent, and that led to my success. When others tried to label me, or expected me to limit myself to my circumstances, I rejected their definitions and decided who and what I would be. Now there is no question about who and what I am. I am a woman. I am a mother. I am a grandmother. I am a teacher. I am a success. I am Doctor Vickie McBride.

Maurice

The people seated around me are smiling as they listen to President McKinney share the short version of my life. They seem impressed that a man who got in trouble when he was young and didn't earn his first degree until he was 30, was now seated among them waiting to be recognized for earning a doctorate. They gasp when they hear the president of the university move on to Vickie's story. When he concludes and asks my mother and me to stand, everyone applauds, and fellow graduates offer their congratulations.

If some of my friends could see me now. I shake my head as I remember the mild shock on some people's faces when they've seen me over the past couple of years. They are amazed that the same high school dropout who used do some of the wild and crazy things I did, is now college-educated. The ones who were with me during my fighting days can't believe the same man who used to walk the streets with them, ready to fight at the slightest provocation, is now legitimately employed and advising young adults to stay on the straight and narrow path. They are amazed, and at times, I am, too. I guess sometimes you have to live it to be able to preach against it.

When I began this journey, my goal was two-fold: to put as much distance between me and my past as possible, and to put myself in a position to fight for the downtrodden, disregarded, and discarded members of society. The fact that I was able to take this step with my mother makes the moment extra special. I forgive her for the harm she did to me. I have apologized for the part I played in our troubles, and she has done the same. We still butt heads sometimes, but she is my mother and I will always love her. Our relationship is probably as close as it has been since I was a small child, and I really hope that it continues to improve.

Receiving adulation from other newly designated doctors waiting to be hooded is a humbling experience. People used to clap for me when I performed on stage; now they were clapping for me as I prepared to cross the stage. I reflect on the last few years and know that, without the presence of God in my life, I would have been in a completely different place — a much worse place. There is no doubt about it. I thank Him silently, over and over again. I thank Him for my mama's enduring faith and unconditional love, for my wife's steadfast loyalty and unrivaled support, and for all of the people along my path who looked at me and saw more than what I was; they saw what I could be. I thank Him for His boundless grace, and for His infinite mercy. I thank Him for being a God of second, third, and fourth chances. I thank Him for my life — a life I sometimes question the existence of because of how it came to be. Yet, I am here. Thank God, I am here!

I was almost a statistic, but became a positive example instead. Despite what people tried to label me, I fought to be something greater. They labeled me a menace; I became someone's help. They labeled me a dropout; I took another route to academic success. They labeled me a felon and bet on my recidivism; I became a poster child for reform. They labeled me a repeat offender; I repeatedly graduated from college and became a doctor that advocates for those who want to make a change but are caught up in an unjust system. Doing these things has taught me that, *despite my label, I am able.* I am able to do all things through Jesus Christ and because of Him. Instead of being what they called me, I am what God made me. I am a man. I am a son. I am a husband. I am a college graduate. I am an author. I am Doctor Maurice McBride.

Acknowledgements

Special thanks to my four children, Dr. Maurice McBride, Jon Desmond McBride-Owens, Avia Parisha McBride-Johnson, and Mark O'Brien Johnson, Jr. – you are my motivation and reason for pushing forward to leave a legacy upon which future generations can build. To my wonderful grandchildren who are the living and breathing reasons I had to take this journey: This is what success looks like if you believe in yourself as I believe in each of you.

I must also acknowledge the late Mattie L. McBride, the late Sammie J. Loftin, the late Don C. McBride, Sr., Alzita Miller, and Martha Golden for standing by me during tough times in my life. Because of each of you, I was able to hold my head high and face motherhood with a positive perspective.

Ruby Morton-Gourdine, thank you for giving me guidance and support when, at just 13 years of age, I had to make the hardest decision of my life and be the mother that my son deserved by setting the example he would need to be successful in life. I will forever be grateful to you for your sacrifice. Thank you to Karen Rubrecht who supported and pushed me to the end by reminding me that I couldn't give up so close to the finish line.

Lastly, I acknowledge all of the young ladies in our society who have taken the journey of single-motherhood and have faced the challenge with optimism and enthusiasm about your futures. I know your struggle, and I have fought your fight. Don't allow your situation to define you; define your situation.

- *Vickie M. McBride, Ph.D.*

I must acknowledge God for allowing me to live this life. Thank you, Father, for Your son Jesus Christ, and for seeing the best in me when everyone else seemed to see the worst.

To my mother Vickie, this story wouldn't have been possible without you. It's been rough, but in the words of Maya Angelou, I "wouldn't take nothing for my journey now."

To my wife Dr. Jessica McBride, who loved me enough to write this book, you are an incredible woman with an amazing talent. The hours you spent listening to our story and crafting it into something wonderful is a labor of love that I will always appreciate. I love you to life!

To my grandmother Mattie Lee McBride (Mama), I pray that you look down from heaven and are proud of both my mother and me, knowing that your efforts were not in vain. You live on in my heart.

Lastly, I acknowledge Dr. Ruby Saxon Myles, Peggy White, and all of the people who helped me along the way whose names are too numerous to list here. Your presence in my life may have been big or small, but if you tried to build me up instead of tear me down, I appreciate you. When naysayers looked at me and saw something bad, you knew that, although I may have been acting like a common worm, I was really a caterpillar that could eventually grow into a butterfly if I just had a safe place to transform. Thank you for providing that cocoon.

- Maurice A. McBride, Ph.D.
on Twitter: @DrMMcBride

Dr. Maurice McBride's Rules for Success

I've been asked many times, "How did you do it, Dr. McBride?" Simply put, there are a few rules that I live by. Maybe you can use some of them to help you when the going gets a little tough.

1. Always try to put God first. I say "try" because even I sometimes failed to do that. However, the consequences of that failure to do so always had a terrible outcome. My belief and faith in God is the only thing that helped me put my life back on track, so get to know Him personally if you don't already.

2. Procrastination is your worst enemy. I often hear people make plans, or say that they are going to get this or that accomplished. However, until you actually turn plans or ideas into action, you will never reach the goals that you aspire to reach. Laziness produces nothing. Go hard or go homeless!

3. Forgiveness is paramount. It takes too much energy to keep holding grudges. The people that you hold grudges against have control over you, so learn from the past, live now, and let it go. This especially holds true when it comes to family.

4. If you do what you have always done, you will get what you have always gotten. So if you want something different, do something different. You can't continue to live the same lifestyle and expect a different outcome.

5. Strive to be different in a positive way. If you do what everyone is doing, then you are nothing more than a carbon copy of the original. Don't be afraid to be bold. Stand out and stand firm. Believe in yourself when no one else does.

6.Your time is your most value asset. No one knows how much time they have left in the "time bank." Therefore, spending it wisely is very important. You should never knowingly let anyone waste your time. It can never be replaced.

7. Be a good listener. The person that knows everything, knows nothing. You'll learn more by listening than talking.

8. If you do what you are supposed to do, when you are supposed to do it, then one day you will be able to do what you want to do, when you want to do it. School isn't the only key to success, but it does help to even the playing field. If you don't have the tools to compete in today's job market, then you will never be considered for the job you want. Try to learn something new every day.

9. Live your life to your fullest potential. Never turn down the opportunity to experience something new. You'll never know if you like it unless you try it. (Proceed with caution and within reason.)

10. You never know how tough you are, until tough is all that you have left. God is my strength that renews me when I'm weak. Rely on Him. There will be many people that will try to discourage you and convince you that you're a failure. Sometimes it will be friends, sometimes it will be family. Stay focused on your goal.

Made in the USA
Columbia, SC
14 February 2025

53799984R00089